RICHARD BURGIN
A LIFE IN VERSE

RICHARD BURGIN
A LIFE IN VERSE

Diana Lewis Burgin

Slavica Publishers, Inc.

Slavica publishes a wide variety of scholarly books and textbooks on the languages, peoples, literatures, cultures, history, etc. of the USSR and Eastern Europe. For a complete catalog of books and journals from Slavica, with prices and ordering information, write to:

>Slavica Publishers, Inc.
>PO Box 14388
>Columbus, Ohio 43214

ISBN: 0-89357-196-2.

Copyright © 1988 by Diana L. Burgin. All rights reserved.

Typeset by Brenda D. Sens.

Printed in the United States of America.

To the memory of my father

TABLE OF CONTENTS

Page

DEDICATION 11
CHAPTER ONE: CHILDHOOD 13
CHAPTER TWO: BOYHOOD 39
CHAPTER THREE: YOUTH 63
CHAPTER FOUR: FIRST LOVE 85
CHAPTER FIVE: THE FINNISH CONNECTION 110
CHAPTER SIX: THE SCANDINAVIAN SEPARATION 137
CHAPTER SEVEN: IN THE NEW WORLD 163
CHAPTER EIGHT: DOUBLE CONCERTO 192
Glossary of Names 220
Source Materials 228

LIST OF ILLUSTRATIONS

1. Josef Joachim's letter 28
2. Lily, Richard, and Bernard Burgin 31
3. Richard as a boy 37
4. Richard Burgin in 1908 65
5. The Fauré Program 100
6. Richard Burgin in 1912 114
7. The Burgins in 1911 126
8. The Burgin String Quartet, 1918 149
9. Richard Burgin upon arrival in the U.S.A. 166
10. Richard Burgin in the 1930s 191
11. Ruth Posselt, 1929 200
12. Richard Burgin and Donna Diana 219

FOREWORD

In the beginning of January, 1981, my father, Richard Moiseevich Burgin, former concertmaster and associate conductor of the Boston Symphony Orchestra, suffered a speech-destroying stroke while playing bridge near his home in St. Petersburg, Florida. A Russian Jew born in Warsaw in 1893, and educated at the Petersburg Conservatory of Music (from which he graduated in 1912, a Silver Laureate in the Silver Age), Richard Moiseevich was cosmopolitan, assimilated, somewhat of a polyglot, but withall, a native speaker of Russian. Through his unspoken, and probably uncalculating influence, I was lured to study that language and literature, and, ultimately, became a Slavist. In this manner of speaking, my life came out of his.

Richard Moiseevich was a fine raconteur, and himself the subject of countless stories, the majority of which discoursed on his absent-mindedness, or bemusement. He would always insist to me, however, that he "never forgot anything important." I wonder. In any case, he lived his long life almost wholly within the oral tradition: never recorded as a soloist or conductor; rarely wrote a letter; scribbled only in his stock books; and left behind a dozen or so empty diaries.

There was no small irony in his end. Not only did his stroke deprive him of speech, it occurred precisely one day after I had bought a tape recorder and he had agreed, with secret pleasure (or so I thought), to let me record his "memoirs." His death (in April, 1981) realized the metaphor and double entendre of his life—he became absent/minded, eluded recording, eluded me.

In the months following his stroke, I plunged into re-searching his life, trying to re-member it. I was most interested, for obvious reasons, in recovering what, in my literary-historical fashion I called his Petersburg period. In the process of research Burgin began to acquire the aura of a Petersburg hero (the model of which is, of course, Pushkin's Eugene Onegin), if not a superfluous, then a super-fluid man, supremely ever-flowing. . .away from me.

By October of 1982 I had gathered a file-drawer full of strikingly heterogeneous information about Richard Burgin, yet I still had no idea in what form to inform anyone about his life. Nevertheless, one evening that fall I sat down to write. My first several pages of biographical prose sounded at best bad, at worst, sad, in a word, not at all as Richard Burgin had sounded to me.

'But how did he sound?' I asked myself in near despair. 'Well,' I mused, 'often he sounded...avuncular, like an uncle full of, full of...what? "Most honest principals? [*Moj djadja samykh chestnykh pravil?*]" How hard that first line of *Eugene Onegin* is to translate! "My uncle of most honest principals,/ when he fell seriously ill,"...."*Moj djadja*...," My papa... no! too childish, too sentimental. Better, "My father," "My father full of..." "My father, full of marvelous stories, at eighty-seven had a stroke, and left untold the joys and worries he'd lived, of which he rarely spoke."'

I seemed to have caught the sound and rhythm of Burgin in the Onegin stanza (14 lines, iambic tetrameter, with fem/MASC rhymes: aBaBccDDeFFeGG). What resulted is the present work. It cannot be called a biography of Richard Burgin; rather it is an imaginative work based in part on Burgin's life and reminiscences up to 1943 and in part on my reading of it and them.

My "Life in Verse" is related to Pushkin's "Novel in Verse" in a number of ways, some obvious, and others more subtle. As the dedicatory stanza suggests, *Richard Burgin*, like *Eugene Onegin*, is a heterogeneous personal narrative poem in eight chapters, each with an epigraph (or two, or three). Its chapters, unlike Pushkin's, however, have titles. The first three are deliberately borrowed from Tolstoy (*Childhood*, *Boyhood*, *Youth*) and the fourth (*First Love*) comes from Turgenev. After Burgin leaves Russia, half-way through the poem, the titles of the chapters of his *Life* no longer have resonance in Russian literature, although some of the events narrated do.

The respective "plots" of *Eugene Onegin* and *Richard Burgin* diverge for the most part, although there are points of contact and deliberate reversal. Where the plot of Pushkin's novel ostensibly revolves around the fictional life, character, unhappy love, and ultimate defeat of the Petersburg dandy, Eugene Onegin, the content of my *Life* concerns the character, profession, loves, and real and imagined life of the Russian-American violinist, Richard Burgin.

Both *Richard Burgin* and *Eugene Onegin*, develop in counterpoint to their external narratives, through the relationship between the poetic "I" and her/his muse, the meta-literary, inner story of how the work came to be written. And so, my "serious burlesque" plays upon certain stylistic aspects of *Eugene Onegin*: digressiveness, the influence of Byron, multi-voicedness, the poet's "life in verse," his/her mid-life crisis, and anxieties of authorship.

But I have no pretensions to being Pushkin, or even a second Pushkin. In the end, what is Pushkin to me, or I to Pushkin? Pushkin is the "father of Russian literature," and I am a daughter of the realm, so to speak, a reader of his novel and a writer of my *Life*. That *Life* began with a dying father at a loss for words, and ends with a birthing daughter who has found them. The ways in which *Richard Burgin* echoes, parallels, polemicizes with, and re/verses its parent text, *Eugene Onegin*, reveal its play upon genre, gender, and generation.

Diana Lewis Burgin

Cambridge, Massachusetts
June, 1988

ANNOTATIONS

All but the universally known of the several real-life and fictional personages referred to in the text are starred (*). Information about them can be found in the alphabetically arranged Glossary of Names at the end. Other items requiring annotation are footnoted and explained at the bottom of the page on which they occur.

The majority of Burgin's recollections, thoughts, and anecdotes which appear in my text as direct quotations represent more-or-less literal "versiphrases" of his own words as spoken during an interview with Professor Elias Dann of Florida State University in 1974. Professor Dann graciously sent me copies of the tapes of this interview shortly after my father's death.

"From early childhood to the end of his eighty-seven years, Richard Burgin's life was marked by those qualities of warmth, humor, curiosity, imagination, generosity, and kindness that stand as hallmarks of a cultured, civilized man, an unforgettable figure who will always remain one of the giants in the history of the Boston Symphony Orchestra."

Steven Ledbetter, *BSO Newsletter*, Summer, 1981.

> *Art is an endless access to revelatory states of mind, a vast extension of living experience and a way of communing with the dead. An intimacy with truth, through which, however much instruction is provided and absorbed, each of us must pass alone.*
>
> Shirley Hazzard

Not heeding savage Death's intrusion,
with live communion in view,
I wished to narrate an illusion
of life far worthier of you,
more worthy of your silent passion,
your fatherly bequest to me,
expressed in true poetic fashion,
with beautiful simplicity;
but that's beyond me—with compassion
accept these strophes Oneginesque,
half-anecdotal, half-scholastic,
purely factual, fantastic,
the fruits of serious burlesque,
long sweats, and sudden inspirations,
the jetsam of my middle years,
a conscious cynic's observations,
and true believer's heartfelt tears.

CHAPTER ONE: CHILDHOOD

And the echo stayed inside the violin...

- Annensky

I.

'My father, full of marvelous stories,
at eighty-seven had a stroke,
and left untold the joys and worries
he'd lived, of which he rarely spoke.
His reticence evoked adorement,
but, oh, my goodness, what a torment
to realize I would never know
the life he played pianissimo.
What unbelievable frustration -
to guess at what was left unsaid,
to learn most relatives were dead
who might confirm my inspiration,
to muse and question in remorse:
How could I fail to ask my source!'

II.

Thus railed a Slavist and professor,
when starting her biography,
by Fantasy's mirage possessor
of papa's Russian legacy.
Friends of Nastásiya and Myshkin!*
With thumping heart I take the risk in
offering my *Life* to you;
its hero is a Russian Jew
named Burgin, my beloved father;
in Petersburg he spent his youth,
a period I've tried to sleuth
or re-imagine, as you'll gather.
(I wanted to be scholarly,
but facts, alas, eluded me.)

III.

A man of cheerful disposition,
and music-loving artisan,
his father labored on commission
in Warsaw for his growing clan.
Although Moisey was enterprising,
it really isn't too surprising,
that with so many mouths to feed,
the Burgins often were in need.
In nineteen five their situation
became unprecedently bad,
and Moses, facing ruin, had
to look for work in emigration. . .
But here, it seems, I've jumped the gun,
so back to Moishe's first-born son!

IV.

He, by family tradition,
was fated for the rabbinate,
and taking on the boy's tuition,
his grandpa tried to inculcate
in him a love for Talmud, Torah,
the meaning of the diaspóra. . .
In vain. To things rabbinical
the boy was often cynical.
He might have realized the division
between his grandpa's Judaism
and his mother's atheism,
and thus resisted all religion;
or maybe he already felt
another calling in himself.

V.

Of this he gave an indication -
at least according to his niece,
whose anecdotal information
came from her mother, now deceased -
when at a concert (so she told her),
a general tapped his father's shoulder,
and said 'Your boy beats time so true,
you'd think he were conducting too!'
Indeed, the child had caught the rhythm,
and waved his arms, completely charmed;
his father gazed at him, disarmed,
but glad he'd brought the child with him,
for when he saw the aforesaid,
he thought, 'My Lord! He's talented!'

VI.

O wondrous tales of Wunderkinder!
I love your truth apocryphal!
Not only do your lies not hinder
my faith in the exceptional,
they bolster it. Exaggeration
itself becomes an explanation
of giftedness my mind may doubt,
but which at heart I know about.
And on a note less introspective,
the lives of Jewish soloists,
the Heifetzes and Zimbalists,
from an historical perspective,
provide a useful way to gauge
the spirit of the Silver Age.

VII.

A frantic time when oh-so-teeny
prodigies were all the rage,
and hoping for a Paganini,
their parents pushed them on the stage,
as if enacting a libretto
entitled Fiddler From the Ghetto.
The drama reached a fever pitch
at Heifetz's appearance, which
made *such* a furious sensation
that it aroused concupiscence
in parents of the audience,
who ringing with the huge ovation,
rushed home afire to see if maybe
they couldn't make another baby.[1]

VIII.

But I digress. Once he'd detected
the certain signs of talent in
his son, our good Moisey collected
some funds to buy a violin,
and then set out to find a teacher
for his gifted little creature.
At last he found one, first of three,
a fiddler named Wiśniewski. He
was in the Warsaw Philharmonic,
and also taught; but practicing
for him exceeded everything -
a kind of life-enhancing tonic -
for when his other work was done,
he'd practice, practice, just for fun!

---

[1] The source of this anecdote was Mischa Piastro, violinist, colleague, and close friend of Richard Burgin at the Petersburg Conservatory. Piastro told it to him after returning from Berlin, where he had the 'misfortune' of making his debut the season after Heifetz's.

IX.

So Richard started taking lessons.
He loved his teacher and progressed
so fast that after several sessions
Wiśniewski made a strange request:
'*Pan*[1] Burgin, it does seem a pity,
although we live in the same city,
I can't teach Richard every day.
And so, might I suggest a way
for him to practice more intensely?
I wonder if you would agree
to let him come and live with me.
His playing would improve immensely,
for pupils need a teacher more
when doing homework than before.'

X.

Moisey agreed, and it transpired,
that he consulted with his spouse,
and they, with high ambitions fired,
sent Richard to Wiśniewski's house.
His six months there of education
instructed him in aspiration,
in practicing with metronome,
and feeling home away from home.

....
....
....
....
....
....

---

[1] *Pan* = Mister (Polish)

XI.

But very likely he was lucky,
in learning how to practice young;
I'd like to have seen him—eager, plucky,
left elbow in, right arm outflung,
lips pursed in zealous concentration,
perfecting the coordination
between his left hand fingerings
and right-arm strokes upon the strings;
eyes scrunched in pure exasperation,
when having got the bowing right,
he'd hear a somewhat more than slight
mistake he'd made in intonation;
the reddening callous on his chin
from practicing the violin.

XII.

Three years he studied with Wiśniewski,
and when he had a little time,
he started reading Dostoevsky...
(here truth *is* sacrificed to rhyme -
though not entirely, for reading
became for him a game exceeding
the other kinds of sports and toys
that usually interest little boys.)
But books were not his only leisure
amusement and activity;
he showed a real proclivity
for playing cards, an utter pleasure,
alike for father and for son,
particularly when they won.

XIII.

O Burgins! Not for lust or fashion
are you distinguished as a *rod*![1]
Your rumpled look bespeaks the passion
of scores exceeded, bids o'ershot
at bridge. What sets your hearts a-thumping?
Why, dealing, bidding, slamming, trumping!
And north, or south, or east, or west,
a long suit makes you look the best.
But now this 'whistful' peroration
has played its hand and worn me out;
besides, I've more to tell about
my hero's early education.
Phase two began when suddenly,
Wiśniewski went to Germany.

XIV.

Yet his replacement wasn't fated
to fill the pedagogic gap;
a stern man, whom kind Moses ''hated''
(because one day he saw him slap
his son for faulty intonation),
he soon gave in his resignation.
I quote: ''If someone hit a child,
why, that would drive my father *wild*!
He once, you know, approached a stranger,
a total stranger about to beat
his son for playing in the street.
'Hey you!' he shouted, 'you're in danger
if you so much as lay a hand...'
and gave the man a reprimand.''[2]

---

[1] *rod* (pronounced 'rot') = clan (Russian).
[2] Richard Burgin (Dann tapes)

XV.

The final member of the triad
of Richard's teachers, no doubt you'll
have heard of: Lotto,* much admired
exponent of the Massart school.
A naturally gifted virtuoso,
whose mental health was only so-so,
he toured through Europe, won renown,
but then, apparently, broke down.
He quit his career concertizing,
returned to Warsaw, where he taught;
his method, Burgin later thought,
"would seem to us today surprising."
(His words were taped by Mr. Dann;*
I'll versify them, if I can.)

XVI.

I quote in full since Truth's my motto,
but since my muse works in reverse,
I must his memories of Lotto
rephrase somewhat to fit her verse,
while trying to retain their flavor,
each crumb of which I really savor,
especially now the speaker's dead,
and I'm deprived of leavened bread.
I know the rises and reactions
of living conversation's yeast
are missing from my rebaked feast,
but that's the curse of all redactions,
of trying to revive the word
which from a dead man's lips I heard.

XVII.

"Ja! Lotto was the strangest teacher!
At least we'd call him strange today.
He was an artist, not a preacher,
and rarely told you *how* to play.
Instead of any explanation
he'd give a perfect demonstration
of what he wanted; then you would
just imitate him, if you could.
So, often I would practice pieces
which were *way* too hard for me.
There only were two books, you see,
he labeled *Études* and *Caprices* -
that's Kreutzer, first, and Paganin -
he knew of nothing in between!

XVIII.

"There was something else, however,
about his teaching that I'd say
was even stranger. He would never
have more than one pupil a day.
In the morning you'd have a lesson,
eat lunch, then have a second lesson,
and just before the evening meal
you'd give a concert, as if for real.
For that he had a whole procedure -
You come in from another room,
the 'green room,' bow, begin to tune;
you'd play, and he accompanied your
performance on his violin,
and his wife would listen in.

XIX.

"I admired Lotto, loved him dearly,
both for his attitude to me,
and as an artist for his really
phenomenal ability."

....
....
....
....
....
....
....
....
....
....

XX.

The virtuosic expectations
of Maestro Lotto's tutelage
filled Richard with high aspirations
for a career on the stage.
Moisey was pleased with his ambition,
yet knew he was in no position
to help his son financially,
however gifted he might be.
So Moses had one grave misgiving
about the future of his son:
'His talent may be next to none,
but no one else will earn his living!'
Thus passes carefree childhood
with worries over livelihood.

XXI.

And there was reason to be worried:
in Russia, chances for a Jew,
no matter how he worked, or scurried
to get ahead, were very few.
To work or play away from home a
musician needed a diploma,
and only Rubenstein's* would do,
from Petersburg or Moscow U.
Yet, musically, youthful Russia,
aspiring and full of pride,
seemed a poor relative beside
the age's ruling emperess, Prussia,
and reigning king of violin,
Joachim, held court in Berlin.

XXII.

But Petersburg's Professor Auer
had just begun to win a name
as *the* important teaching power
behind the throne of Elman's* fame.
And Petersburg's conservatory
not only gave a chance for glory,
it also granted *the* degree
which guaranteed security.
This fact compelled consideration,
for talents, on the average,
seem less prodigious as they age;
unknown the middle-aged sensation,
and last year's wonder held in awe
becomes this year's "already saw."

XXIII.

Sic transit gloria mundi. True, but
how much we want it all the same!
So much, there's nothing we can do but
(and who will say that we're to blame?)
take up the quest of Kavalérov,*
delight in envy and despair of
achieving an old-fashioned goal:
expense of mind in waste of soul.
Thus parodying literary
examples of superfluousness
we spurn mere moderate success
for failure extra-ordinary.
Yet all of us have learned in school,
exceptions always prove the rule.

XXIV.

Psychologists have said it's female
to want and yet to fear success,
but Russian novels show that *the* male
loves losing too. Hence the excess
of self-destructive Karamazovs,*
Pechorins,* Silvios,* Bazarovs,*
who'd rather leave the task undone,
than risk not being number one;
who far prefer the laceration
of being a superfluous man*
than just another also-ran
content to thrive in moderation;
who, finally, if they can't be best,
would die than live like all the rest.

XXV.

To be or not. That IS the question;
and sometimes being is a bore.
How it vexes, the suggestion,
that's all there is, there ain't no more!
So when you feel you'll never make it,
you're often tempted to forsake it,
while making sure the world out there
will understand you do not care.
It's not success we fear, but failing
to win attention; and here's the proof:
if others worry, you're aloof,
but if they don't, you end up wailing
in gross self-pity, 'Why, oh why,
is *my* lot but to do and die?!'

XXVI.

Some say that talent is a blessing,
while others deem it more a curse,
but one thing's sure, if it's depressing
to have none, some is even worse.
Is sanguine not to sanguinary
as Mozart to his foe, Salieri,*
the poisoner poisoned by his fate
of being good, but second rate?
Recipient of modifiers,
a sufferer of the somewhat-too's,
not-bads, and almost-got-it blues,
he's damned by endless qualifiers
to minuses in front of A's
for being "good in many ways."

XXVII.

Enough! I'll finish this digression,
or I'll run out of things to say,
and worse, reveal my own obsession
with fame, and give myself away.
So to my tale I turn directly,
which, if I can recall correctly,
I left with Moses in a stew
considering what he should do
about young Richard's education:
he weighed the options carefully,
and then consulted endlessly
from fear of some miscalculation.
Whichever course he chose to take,
Richard's future seemed at stake.

XXVIII.

At last he took him to audition
in Petersburg for Auer, who
accepted him without condition,
and offered him a stipend, too.
Of course, good Moses was delighted,
and Richard—terribly excited.
He felt he'd passed his first big test,
and things would turn out for the best.
Yet once back home, upon more sober
reflection, Moses wasn't sure;
Berlin still had its old allure,
so when he went there in October
of nineteen two, just on a whim
he took his son along with him.

XXIX.

'Perhaps,' he thought, 'our luck will hold and
Joachim, though a famous man,
will deign to hear my nine-year-old and
agree to help him, if he can.
It's worth a try,' concluded Moses,
'for man decides, but Chance disposes.'
(Adhering to this principle,
he reconciled fate with will.)
In this case Burgin's intuition
proved amply justified. Indeed,
Joachim readily agreed
to give the youngster an audition.
That hearing in Charlottenburg
surpassed the one in Petersburg.

XXX.

Of this there's written confirmation:
a letter which Joachim wrote,[1]
containing an evaluation
of Richard's talent. Let me quote:
he "certif[ies]...the boy possesses
a genuine gift," and then expresses
his "real surprise at the aplomb
with which the child played Vieuxtemps.
He merits serious instruction,
and with a talent such as this,
steps should be taken to resist
that most exploitative seduction
of forcing him upon the stage
before he's musically of age."

---

[1] Dated October 4, 1902. Original in German.

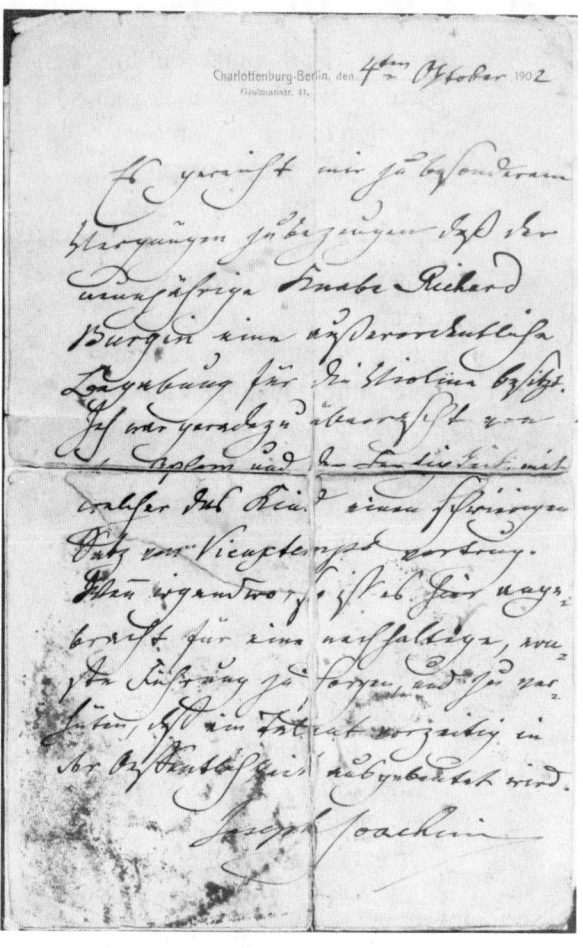

Josef Joachim's letter evaluating nine-year-old Richard's talent.

XXXI.

Joachim said he would be willing
to teach the youngster privately.
For Moses this was simply thrilling,
but money worried him, and he
replied 'Professor, I'm so sorry,
there's no way I could pay.' 'Don't worry,'
Joachim soothed his visitor,
'I'll see he's well-provided-for.
I'll get some funds, and ask my distant
relations living in Berlin,
if they could take young Richard in,
and he will work with my assistant,
Markees, and every month, you see,
I'll have him come and play for me.'

XXXII.

So it was settled, and my Richard
left home before the age of ten
to start a life in earnest which had
been just a wild dream till then.
But since his years away from Poland
contain another story, whole and
complete within itself, I, too,
shall put it off till chapter two,
and finish one with speculations
on what my prodigy was like
when he was just a little tyke:
what might have been his expectations?
how did he act? how did he look?
what *was* the childhood he forsook?

XXXIII.

I've seen an early childhood picture
of Richard, with Lily and Bernard,
his siblings. It betrays a mixture
of youth and fatherly regard:
his hand upon his brother's shoulder
and look of worry make him older,
but his paternal mien can't hide,
in fact reveals, the child inside.
O first-born child! Your emulation
of parents satisfies a wish
to be grown up, a childish
desire for grown-ups' adulation.
How innocent and worldly-wise
the *puer senex's* disguise!

XXXIV.

I know this since I played at mother
from five or six years old, I guess,
and helped bring up my younger brother,
to my great pride, and his distress.
But there's a crucial differential
between the parenting potential
of him and me; I gave it up
as child's play when I grew up,
whereas my hero's urge paternal
was not a role, but an innate
proclivity, the sort of trait
that Dostoevsky called "eternal,"
for he would father all his life
his siblings, children, friends, and wife.

From left to right: Lily, Richard, and Bernard Burgin, about 1899.

XXXV.

And thus, when I have seemed alone in
the world, I have most strongly felt,
there *muss ein lieber Vater wohnen*,
somewhere above the *Sternenzelt*.
At least, I wished to feel most strongly,
for Beethoven could not have wrongly
harmonized an "Ode to Joy"
that even death cannot destroy.
"*O Freude!* Soul of all creation!
O Tochter aus Elysium!
Whenceforth, o daughter, have you come?"
Are you not Death's transfiguration,
who rose when Mother Ceres wise
effected there a compromise?

XXXVI.

Alas! I see that what I've written
till now about my soloist
contains a flaw, and I am smitten
with guilt sincerely feminist.
I've spoken of my Richard's father,
but seem to have ignored his mother.
Although the gap's intolerable,
perhaps it may be fillable.
The problem is that very little
about his mother is known to me;
it seems her friends and family
regarded Ronia as a riddle,
because she rarely ever said
the half of what was in her head.

XXXVII.

Perhaps she was a *gentle creature*,*
in talk subdued, in silence strong.
For Moses, her outstanding feature
was *not* to speak when he was wrong,
and in her silent disapproval
he often heard a stern reproval.
With talk, he was the opposite,
and could not get enough of it.
And theirs was not a happy marriage:
by blood and passion they were tied,
but in all other things they vied,
the good old saw I shan't disparage:
it's true that opposites attract,
yet joined, they seldom interact.

XXXVIII.

And thus we have these loving cousins
whose marriage was a battleground.
She was a loner; he liked dozens
of people always milling 'round;
about belief she could be caustic,
he half believed, a mild agnostic;
her politics were radical,
and his far more canonical;
and Moses was the more dogmatic -
at heart he felt the urge to teach -
while Ronia, who would never preach,
was probably more charismatic.
Her children spoke of her with awe,
and took her silent word as law.

XXXIX.

But still, they somehow worked together
in forming Richard's character.
It's hard to say with sureness whether
he took more after him or her:
for Ronia he had great compassion,
but clearly shared his father's passion
for music, cards, and company;
he loved his parents equally,
and when at times he felt suspended
between their views, unconsciously,
he strove for peace and harmony,
on which his happiness depended.
He sought to please with diligence
both members of his audience.

XL.

By nature proud, an overreacher,
he often saw himself to blame
where others might rebuke their teacher,
and in this way he overcame
the urge for childish rebellion,
aspired to angel, scorned the hellion,
squelched his wants, his feelings hid,
and overdid what he was bid.
Of course, no child could have voted,
at *that* time, in the long debate
between his parents on his fate.
About their choice he later noted,
"It was a toss-up in a way,
but either way, I had no say."

XLI.

So, was his childhood good and happy?
Or did it bring him pain and grief?
The question is both moot, and sappy -
all I can say is, it was brief.
And has my *Childhood* been inspired?
Or has it grievously misfired?
I do not know, but good or bad,
too short or long, too gay or sad,
I can't be blamed. My muse parental
has called the shots. I had no choice,
but try to give her wishes voice;
like Richard's mine were incidental.
In what would finally be heard
I was not seen to have a word.

XLII.

We're dutiful, we sons and daughters
of conscience's modality;
our childish 'wills' with ádult 'oughtas'
we still before maturity.
But early on we learn repression
can be a form of self-expression;
that inner voice, 'Thou shalt not shirk,'
awakens real desire—for work,
and work is the most gratifying
of pleasures. Though you must forego
some others for it, still I know
no *jouissance* less self-denying:
it isn't like the birds and bees
where often one may just not please.

XLIII.

Excessive work may be neurotic,
like nymphomania, drugs, or booze,
but it can also be erotic
in self-fulfillment or -abuse.
The urge to work! so strong, seductive,
the stimulus to be productive,
will get you up and out of bed,
and powerfully turn your head
away from everything. Forgotten
are food, drink, friends, and pet bow-wow;
aroused, you've got to do it now,
and well-conceived or misbegotten,
you do not care because the fun
is in the doing, not the done.

XLIV.

And there's the rub. Post-work depression
is similar to little death;
hence, the last gasp of this digression,
but now, I'm running out of breath,
and suffering from rhyme occlusion,
which forces an abrupt conclusion.
Of chapter one there'll be no more;
besides, I've got a date at four,
it's nearly three, the dog needs walking,
I've yet to wash, or comb my hair,
and still must finish *The Corsair*,
about which we shall all be talking
tonight at Janet's. So, adieu,
we'll meet again in chapter two.

Richard as a boy.

CHAPTER TWO: BOYHOOD

1

Ach, Berlin!
Oh, yarn!

I.

My yarn continues in the city
where Richard spent his boyhood years,
Berlin, which then was sitting pretty
at music's center; its two ears,
the Petersburgian Polaris
and westerly Venusian Paris,
were stars of secondary size
in European music's skies.
In France the new impressionism
refracted the Teutonic beam,
while Russia sparkled in the gleam
of German post-Wagnerianism.
Effulgence of Berlin shone bright
in rival and reflected light.

II.

The concerts of the Philharmonic
were under Nikisch's baton,
a master of technique symphonic,
and post-romantic paragon.
The *Oper* thrived on strong sensations
of fatal feminine vocations:
the Queen of Spades' malicious play;
the heady dance of Salomé.
The Kaiser thought the last so vampish,
he pitied Strauss and moaned "*Mein Gott*!
I like this fellow quite a lot,
but this, I fear, will do him damage!"
"The damage," later noted Strauss,
"made possible my Garmisch house."[1]

III.

When Strauss, the age's Great Composer,
had reached the apex of his fame,
my Richard, still in *Lederhosen*,
knew little of him but his name.
Yet, sensitive to all vibrations
which echoed in his generation's
development in old Berlin,
unwittingly he took Strauss in,
although, at ten, he'd not suspected
that he would meet the man one day,
and under his direction play
the poem which his life reflected,
Ein Heldenleben's solo *Streich*[2]
shall vibrate through my hero's life.

---

[1] Harold Schoenberg, *Lives of the Great Composers*.
[2] *Streich* = string (German).

IV.

Nor had he any expectation,
that half a century later, he
would lead *Death and Transfiguration*[1]
with the Boston Symphony;
nor that his daughter would try to capture
his life through that remembered rapture,
or turn to articles on Strauss
to coax Berlin's *Zeitgeist heraus*,
or ponder tomes in Harvard College
Music Library, sigh, and think,
'Perhaps I've found some sort of link
in Maitland[2] with Joachim, knowledge
than can in part evoke those times,
if only I can find the rhymes.'

V.

No, Richard's thoughts were more mundane and
appropriate to a ten-year-old
confronted by a strange terrain and
adjustment to a new household.
At first it all seemed quite bewildering,
but when he got to know the children
of his family in Berlin,
he felt at home and fit right in.
He quickly learned *die deutsche Sprache*,
im Hause spielend[3] spent his days,
and started lessons with Markees;
each month or so he'd see Joachim,
who checked his progress carefully,
and treated him most fatherly.

---

[1] *Death and Transfiguration* was conducted by Richard Burgin with the Boston Symphony several times. The performance recalled here took place in November, 1962.
[2] Maitland, biographer of Josef Joachim.
[3] *die deutsche...* = the German language,/at home playing

VI.

Joachim, when my Richard knew him,
was past the age of seventy,
but had begun (as critics view him)
an archetypal prodigy.
He had debuted when he was seven,
and then, a youngster of eleven,
he "captivated" Mendelssohn,
and went to England where he won
what proved a lasting reputation.
The sounds of Beethoven and Brahms
contained for Josef special charms;
renowned for his interpretation
of their concerti, he composed
cadenzas every fiddler knows.

VII.

In 'sixty nine appointed rector
of Berlin's High School *für Musik*,[1]
Joachim was a great respector
of tonal art above technique.
His study of articulation
and difficulties of notation
in Back—when to or not to slur -
in pedagogy made a stir.
To florid style antipathetic,
he challenged the Romantic taste
for showiness, with programs based
more on a Classical aesthetic;
and finally (how could I forget?!)
he led a world-renowned quartet.

---

[1] *für Musik* = for Music

VIII.

Joachim has received his share of
research and praise, but as regards
his playing, scholars aren't aware of
one side of it: his love of cards.
Burgin once recalled with laughter,
"He'd listen to me play, and after,
he'd say '*Talant hast du recht viel!
Nun, willst einmal' n Kartenspiel?*'[1]
And playing with me gave him pleasure,
you know, since I was very good
at cards. From earliest childhood,
it was my favorite form of leisure...
Ja! He was wonderful to me,
just liked me, and played cards with me."

IX.

Markees had none of these attractions,
as we from Burgin's memories cull:
"I had begun to have reactions
to teachers, and, I found him dull.
He was, I guess, a bit scholastic,
and so, to make my wrist elastic,
he had me practice every day
a Bach sonata the strangest way;
for several months that seemed unending,
I had to hold my right hand close
to a chair, you see, be forced
to play just with my wrist, and bending
my fingers, crossing strings, you know,
Dee-da, dee-da—just with the bow.

---

[1] *Talent hast du...* = You're really very talented. Now how about a game of cards?

X.

"But later, I appreciated
what this Markees has tried to do,
and also, to be educated,
I think one needs some strictness, too.
A certain discipline in study
is very good for anybody;
it was his strictness probably
that gave me flexibility. . .
Outside of Bach, obligatory,
the things I studied were, of course,
études and scales to reinforce
technique; the standard repertory;
and also, I remember, Spohr -
Concerto Two, in *re minor*.

XI.

"That was a different world from Lotto,
a new approach entirely.
Like many French musicians, Lotto
would think of sound pictorially.
For him there always was a story
connected with the auditory,
and whether it was *La Légende*,[1]
or Sarasate, or Vieuxtemps,
the sound evoked associations;
accompanying figures dealt
with what the hero saw or felt
in some specific situations;
there was a plot to be resolved,
you had to *live* it, be involved."

---

[1] *La Légende*, a virtuoso showpiece by Wieniawski.

XII.

In hearing Burgin's commentary
about his training in Berlin,
I'm struck by two quite adversary
approaches to the violin:
first there's Lotto, passion, pictures;
then Markees, restraint, and strictures;
from strokes exultant *en plein air*
to arm held rigid by a chair,
as if (forgive my strange allusion)
a boyish Nástenka-like* flirt
were safety-pinned to grandma's skirt
to check the childlike effusion
of untamed virtuosity
with disciplined sobriety.

XIII.

Ideally they are in conjunction;
in any field of life or art
it's quite impossible to function
with heartless mind or mindless heart.
Unfortunately, that's the trouble,
since every person has a double,
and raging schizophrenia
results in neurasthenia.
How often it becomes exhausting
to find the perfect equipoise
of being-doing, quiet-noise,
Oblomovitizing* and Fausting,
and that's because the middle way
appears discouragingly gray.

XIV.

Untrammelled feeling can be banal,
and in its flabby excess—crass;
but too much discipline is anal,
and in its rigor lacking brass.
To play Bach as the first romantic
will always make the purists frantic,
but when they hear a J. Strauss waltz,
some like a little bit of schmaltz.
To find the manner for the master
is every great performer's goal;
Tchaikovsky thrives on Russian soul,
but soulful Mozart spells disaster;
and Brahms requires seriousness,
but Paganini—playfulness.

XV.

At times a fiery bravura
performance surely fits the bill,
but trying to create a furor
at other times can be quite ill-
advised. I'd like, in this conenction,
to quote a similar reflection
which Burgin made about the part
the soloist should play in art:
"You cannot always be a Hamlet,
and only speak soliloquies,
give personal philosophies,
or by yourself perform the gamut;
you also have to interact
with other players and *react*."

XVI.

I'm sure he meant his words sincerely,
and do not doubt that they are true,
yet, as a boy, I bet he dearly
desired to be a Hamlet too.
He had been dealt at life's beginning
two hands: one losing, the other winning,
a choice—to be or not to be
a genuine child prodigy.
For having Richard learn to diddle
orchestral *tutti* -parts, and strive
for second violin at five,
was *not* why Moses bought a fiddle.
No! his dream was purely singular -
a secret wish upon a star.

XVII.

Stars! Program booklets wax about them,
from glossy pics their faces grin,
and playbills, posters, papers shout them,
regardless of what town you're in.
Berlin, Warszawa, New York City -
all audiences' favorite ditty
is 'Twinkle, twinkle, child star,
how we wonder what you are!'
The child star, however, flashes
but once, at birth; then it's too late
to use its light to navigate,
against the rocks of age one smashes;
and Richard was already ten,
which meant, decision-time again!

XVIII.

Though he himself had little notion
of what eventually he would do,
the time had come to put in motion
arrangements for the boy's debut.
His hometown orchestra provided
its sponsorship; it was decided
the Wunderkind's debut would be
December seventh, nineteen three.
I've always wondered, was he nervous?
and asked my mother if she knew
(she was a "child wonder" too).
She answered, "Children are impervious
to nerves; they think it's all a game
until. . .they're conscious of their fame."

XIX.

Perhaps. But still I have the feeling,
when Richard's big first night arrived,
he must have found it hard concealing
the butterflies he felt inside.
Did he remember Lotto's lessons -
those just-like-real-performance sessions -
when dressed in velvet, collar'd in lace,
with curls encircling his face,
he walked on stage, tuned up, and waited,
a half-size fiddle 'neath his chin,
for his performance to begin?
And at the end, was he elated
to hear words redolent of bliss -
so sweet! so fleeting! - Bravo! Bis!

XX.

A Russian newspaper in Warsaw
Západny gólos ("Western Voice"),
remarked that he "produced a furor,"
which surely made his heart rejoice,
and gave the management a reason
to schedule for the following season
my *virtuoza-skripachá*[1]
with the *Filarmonija*.
But my young Richard's evolution
into performing prodigy
had just begun, when suddenly,
in nineteen five, the Revolution
brought family crisis in its wake,
and undercut his first big break.

XXI.

Moisey's decision to leave Poland
was economic (see *One, III*);
amid upheavals it was *no* land
for business opportunity.
With less incoming than outgoing,
and with his child production showing
no sign of slowing even at six,
Moisey was really in a fix.
In nineteen five his brother Leo[2]
had left and settled in New York;
he wrote to say that he'd found work,
and Moses mused, 'Perhaps you'll be, oh
America, deliverance,
and offer me a second chance.'

---

[1] *virtuoza-skripacha* = virtuoso violinist (Russian)
[2] Leo (Leib) Burgin, one of Moses's three brothers, active in the Polish Worker's movement.

XXII.

So when the Polish situation
became unalterably grim,
Moisey resolved on emigration:
he'd take his oldest son with him
but leave at home his several other
children, and, of course, their mother;
and if his gains should top his loss,
he hoped to bring them all across.
Thus Moses, having expectations,
could fight his slough of deep despond,
but Richard? How did he respond?
With joy? Or had he reservations?
Did he, in fact, prefer to roam
around the world, or stay at home?

XXIII.

The only memories I'm aware of
him having of his German years
were fond: he was "well-taken-care-of,"
enjoyed the friendship of his peers,
liked the family which he stayed with,
and "loved" Joachim whom he played with.
"It was a happy time," he'd tell,
"and with my music I did well."
So probably he felt a spasm
of sorrow when he had to leave;
yet only briefly would he grieve,
since he possessed enthusiasm,
and future dreams so filled his mind
that he could leave the past behind.

XXIV.

What future dreams? For me this poses
a puzzle, and my readership
might also query, why did Moses
take Richard on the new world trip?
I'm forced to guess the explanation:
had he a hidden motivation
to spurn the European fame
already spreading Richard's name?
Had he perhaps become ambitious
to scale the lofty new world heights,
see Richard's name in New York lights,
and hoped the moment was propitious
to launch abroad sensationally
a European prodigy?

XXV.

If so, I think the great sensation
that Richard made was not the kind
by any stretched imagination
that could have entered Moishe's mind.

....
....
....
....
....
....
....
....
....
....

2

New York, New York!
(Popular Song)

XXVI.[1]

I love you, Peter Minuit's purchase,
I love your steel and glass attire;
it seems the vault of heaven perches
atop your tallest Empire spire.
I love your thrust and aspiration,
the grandeur of Grand Central Station,
the tawdry glamor of Times Square,
where gawking tourists stop and stare;
the dazzling costs of your per diems,
the glittering stores where in a thrice
one spends ten times your purchase price;
I love the wealth of your museums,
your theaters, films, but most of all,
I love in you Carnegie Hall.

---

[1] Stanza XXVI parodies the rhythm and diction of Pushkin's well-known paen to the city of St. Petersburg in the Invocation to *The Bronze Horseman*, which begins, "I love you, Peter's creation,/I love your stern, harmonious look [. . .]

XXVII.

My visits there have been infrequent,
yet I'm among its devotees,
because it conjures up both piquant
and poignant family memories.
I think I'll save my own for later,
but one of Richard's forms the greater
proportion of this chapter's end;
first, however, I intend
to give, by way of preparation,
some facts about the New York scene
when Richard came there as a teen,
flesh out contextual narration,
and build up to his memory
through strict sequentiality.

XXVIII.

The concert life in New York City,
during Richard's visit there,
was, judging by my sources, pretty
much the same as anywhere.
The trustees of the Philharmonic
Society engaged Safónov
to keep the orchestra in time
from nineteen six to nineteen nine;
the Russian Orchestra of local
repute premiered Rachmaninov;
Scriabíne, and Rimsky-Korsakov;
and Germans topped the bill in vocal
performance with their very fine
Liederkranz Gesangverein.

XXIX.

Musicians came from many nations -
Germans, Slavs, and Wandering Jews -
the widely recognized sensations,
and hopefuls making their debuts.
The city was a cultural Babel,
but supertalents still were able
to harmonize some rare delights
for musical cosmopolites.
It was a town to test the mettle,
to challenge, realize, or destroy
the dreams of any aspiring boy,
and Richard, though in finest fettle
when he arrived, was struck with awe
by what he heard and what he saw.

XXX.

The rapid, roaring, groaning gliss of
the subway deafened Richard's ears,
but kindly welcome words of Krisoff
soothed his nerves and calmed his fears.
(Krisoff was my hero's other
American uncle, Ronia's brother;
my new arrivals lived with him
at one-five-seven-six Madison).
Once Richard had unpacked and rested,
reset his inner metronome,
and got in time with his new home,
of all his qualms he was divested.
He learned some English, felt much freer,
and set about his new career.

XXXI.

The Music School that was connected
with Liederkranz Society
auditioned Richard and selected
the boy to play as prodigy.
His solos earned him commendation,
as well as some remuneration,
and then, a Mr. Filchscheimér,
who was a wealthy amateur
of chamber music, and was looking
for a fourth, gave him the job.
He'd play quartets and then hobnob,
earn cash, experience, and...good cooking!
He noted, "It was quite a deal -
five dollars an evening, and a meal.

XXXII.

"Those meals there simply were delicious!"
I taste his praises with my eyes;
they whet digressive bits nutritious
to please my palate epic-wise.
O tempting, titillating dinners,
how you beguile us fleshly sinners!
bedevil us with eggs and steak,
diavolos, and chocolate cake!
From soup to nuts we love all courses;
in *haute, midi,* or *basse cuisine
de l'Amérique, la France, ou Chine,*
we eat *comme les chevaux* (like horses).
Yet even when I'm full, *j'ai faim*
for any sort of *pôts de crème.*

XXXIII.

For certain things we all have passions:
Pushkin for feet and Keats for dreams,
Gógol for noses, Byron—fashions,
Swinburne—whips, and Burgin—creams.
*Frappées, glacées, anglaises, françaises,
aux chocolats, vanilles, ou fraises,*
all flavors and varieties
my gustatory organs tease.
A cream is dining's culmination
and at its best if saved for last,
but when I'm rushed and must eat fast,
without a moment's hesitation,
I'll pass the preparatory fare,
and quickly have a cream éclair.

XXXIV.

Yes! cream can make me feel euphoric;
its marvels are past arguing.
I cite its meaning metaphoric:
the choicest part of anything.
The best of crops or social stations,
among the highest approbations,
for what can be one's goal supreme
if not the judgment 'cream of cream'?
And on a more material level -
I'm fond of such antitheses -
cream soda, sauces, puffs, and cheese
are goods in which I also revel.
Indeed, for me, good-better-best
means creamy-creamier-creamiest.

XXXV.

However, though I've hardly sated
my appetite for sweet, rich cream,
I'll end, before I am berated,
and lose my readers' high esteem.
To those who deem my taste egregious
and scream 'Enough!' I say 'Who needs-yuz?'
For those who think my diet extreme,
I recommend a bream regime;
on those who judge my dreams unseemly,
or teem with rage that I blaspheme
an epic theme with anatheme,
I wish digressiveness supremely
beseeming all their watery ilk -
a steady stream of non-fat milk!

XXXVI.

Let's see, where was I? Ah yes, preparing
the climax of this second part
by telling how the boy was faring
professionally in his art.
Besides recitals, Liederkrancing,
and quartets, he did freelancing
in Arnold Volpe's Orchestra,*
and also played the cinema.
Although his state of mind was sunny,
some little clouds began to form
from pressure to exceed the norm
and constant worries over money.
This darkening sky, alas, portends
a musical storm of means and ends.

XXXVII.

The outburst came in nineteen seven,
a gloomy year in Richard's life,
when what had seemed a new-world heaven
was drowned by hellish storm and strife.
The sprinkles started with a panning,
and ended in a downpour, banning
the youngster from the concert stage,
because he still was underage.
In March he gave a big recital,
which drew a small but friendly house,
and made the New York critics grouse.
That hurt, but taught him something vital,
the moral of the concert hall:
in every life some rain must fall.

XXXVIII.

This was an adage he'd remember,
perhaps remember to forget,
when in the deluge of November,
his whole career was upset;
but I distinctly do remember
how I learned of that November...
the Library; oh, my eyes were sore
from scanning microfilms of yore!
My strength was sapped, I felt like napping,
about to mutter, 'Nevermore,
will I peruse forgotten lore,'
when suddenly came Katherine's[1] tapping,
'Diana, look!' I bent, stared hard,
and read: BOY VIOLINIST BARRED

---

[1] Dr. Katherine T. O'Connor, friend and colleague.

XXXIX.

RICHARD BURGIN NOT ALLOWED TO
PLAY WITH VOLPE ORCHESTRA.
(The headlines fit my verse, but how to
convey the rest without faux pas?
It seems I can't make journalism
conform to my poeticism,
so with the effort I'll make done,
and versiphrase the *New York Sun*.)[1]
In brief, before the concert started,
Maèstro Volpe was informed,
that if the Burgin boy performed,
there'd be no concert. He departed
when asked to leave, but once outside,
he heard the concert start, and cried.

XL.

The reasons for the Gerry's[2] hounding
my Richard from the concert stage
would really not have been astounding
had they to do with just his age.
But there was something superseding
that fact, and strangely, it was reading,
or more specifically, a book,
which from the library he took
to read at home, and had forgotten.
When it became long overdue,
they claimed he stole it. (Wouldn't you
agree with me that that was rotten?
Had Widener gotten on my trail
for late returns, I'd be in jail.)

---

[1] *The New York Sun*, November 22, 1907 (front page).
[2] Gerry = The Children's Society

XLI.

In any case, he was arrested,
and then in Children's Court arraigned.
He "pleaded guilty as suggested
by counsel," under oath explained,
in answer to the accusations,
that "ignorant of regulations
in this new land," he never knew
the library book was overdue.
Then Moses made his peroration
as the eternal suppliant:
'Your Honor, I spent every cent
I had on Richard's education.
Now he's the sole support, you see,
of his entire family.'

XLII.

The judge paroled the boy that morning,
but said, 'Tonight you can't appear
at Volpe's concert. Heed my warning,
my boy, or we shall interfere.'
The story came in several versions -
which are true, and which perversions?
The *Sun's* was most detailed by far;
the *Times's* in details bizarre:
"One less musician than expected
appeared last night...and we were told
that Bergmann [*sic*!], fifteen years old,
was banned because his father objected
to his young son's appearance here,
and asked the Gerry to interfere."[1]

---

[1] I might note that in actual fact, Burgin, born on October 11, 1893, was only 14 years old.

XLIII.

I find this last account revealing
despite the "Bergmann"[1] oversight,
because inside I have the feeling
the way it sees Moisey is right.
Knowing Richard, he suspected
that hoping he'd be undetected,
the boy would probably disobey
Judge Wyatt, and attempt to play.
'Is better I should burst his bubble,'
he thought, 'and call this Gerry in
myself then have that court step in
and make for us still more the trouble.
As if I do not got enough
of all this court and legal stuff!'

XLIV.

Moishe's thoughts on intervention
in this regrettable affair
convey an overtone of tension,
perhaps a note of real despair.
Indeed, the city that had fired
his hopes for work and had inspired
his trip away from Warsaw's slough,
appeared far less enchanting now.
His hopes no longer were ascendent,
the work he'd found had been a loss,
for used to being his own boss,
by nature proud and independent,
it seemed that he could not adjust
to working for some giant trust.

---

[1] The name of the banned player, according to the *New York Times* account (November 22, 1907) was "Adolph Bergmann." The incident is also reported by Marie Volpe in her biography of Arnold Volpe (Miami, 1950) on the basis of the account in the *New York World*.

XLV.

Although Moisey had always prided
himself on his tenacity,
on this occasion he decided -
albeit somewhat ruefully -
he was not meant to be a rover,
he could not bring his family over,
the new world way was full of bumps,
and he was really in the dumps;
he'd dug himself into a hole and
no longer had the slightest doubt
for him there was but one way out,
and that was—to return to Poland.
But where would youthful Richard go?
(Just wait! in chapter three you'll know.)

CHAPTER THREE: YOUTH

For he is the artist of his own life...

- Dostoevsky

I.

'So where he go? oy, such a worry!'
'Ach, Leib, I'm really in a state!'
'*Natürlich, Brüder*, and I'm sorry,
but what will be your Richard's fate?'
'Who knows?' 'But Moishe, time is flying,
and what will you accomplish crying?'
'*Da nichevó*.[1] 'I understand
your fears, but take yourself in hand.
The first thing, listen what I'm saying,
you going home, and he with you,
and there, you told me, ist nicht true?
he had success already, playing,
did good, and didn't break no rules;
they got good teachers, music schools...'

II.

'I don't yet see to what you're getting?'
'Why Petersburg! That's what I'd choose.'
'But Leib, you seem to be forgetting
the way things are there now for Jews -
pogróms, and quotas...' 'Ja, and Auer!
Don't he got there a lot of power?
Besides, he heard your Richard play
already, and, did you not say,
he thought him good? Well, now he's better!
So, Moishe, why you look so grim?
Why don't you get in touch with him?'
'We're here, he's there.' 'So write a letter!'
'To Auer?' 'Ja!' 'Now?' 'Right away!
My words you mark, he saves the day!'

---

[1] *Da nichevo* = Well, nothing (Russian).

III.

From Leib's fraternal exhortation,
Moisey got back the pluck he'd lost,
wrote Auer of the situation,
and waited with his fingers crossed.
In six weeks came a letter saying,
'I do recall your Richard's playing,
and if he has not gotten worse,
I will accept him in my course.
To find that out, he must audition;
so I suggest your son you bring
to London, where I am each spring.'
In hope that Leo's intuition
foretold a better future soon,
Moisey and son set sail in June.

IV.

They sailed aboard the Lusitania,
and disembarked at Liverpool;
the tension mounted, hemicrania
made my Richard's blood run cool;
his throat was dry, his heartbeat faster,
he clenched his teeth to try to master
the fits and starts of fear inside
that seemed to orchestrate the ride
to London. Silent terror. Auer's
'When you're ready, please begin.'
He put the fiddle 'neath his chin;
then, forty minutes lasting hours,
it's over—'Thank you'—flash of fright,
'I've failed,' but Auer said, "All right."

Richard Burgin, shortly before his return to Warsaw in June, 1908. The inscription on the back reads: *Dem Onkel Leo, Zum Andenken an die New-Yorker Tage vervleibe ich, Dein Neffe Richard Burgin 27.V.08.*

V.

So now I must be off to Peter
to recompose my hero's youth;
the city, famed in Pushkin's meter,
and Dostoevsky's prosey truth;
the city, both mundane and magic,
grotesquely comic, nobly tragic,
the source of Russian national myth,
Germanic, foreign, native Scyth-
ian, the real and legendary
battleground of West and East,
both New Jerusalem and Beast,
was then in an extraordinary
destructively-creative stage,
the climax of the Silver Age.

VI.

An urgency apocalyptic,
a desperate yearning for the strange,
the new and ancient, mystic-cryptic,
gripped Russia in the throes of change.
Everywhere raged controversy;
the bourgeoisie now pleaded mercy,
now underwrote its reeling shock,
supporting artists run amok
with innovations real and phony,
transgressing proper boundaries,
destroying decent harmonies
with mystic chords and cacophóny,
expressing the creative molt
of Russian culture in revolt.

VII.

The eighteen nineties' dying flower
of decadent aestheticism
reblossomed in Ivanov's* Tower
as symbolistic mysticism;
the poets seeking God and gnosis
saluted their apotheosis
in sound, from which the Word arose:
De la musique avant toute chose!
And striving for transcendence via
the myth Prometheus Unbound,
in symphony of light and sound
Scriabin* proclaimed himself messiah,
resolving all antitheses
in monumental syntheses.

VIII.

His music sang the aspiration
of culture that was all at odds;
in spastic self-disintegration,
it sought the twilight of the gods,
that would consume reactionaries,
as well as revolutionaries,
and reconcile Bolshevists
with anarchists and monarchists;
resolve dichotomistic preachings -
Lev Tolstoy's arch-purity
and Saninesque* depravity -
and overreach the overreachings
of every artist's separate part,
in one transcendent world of art.*

IX.

The world of Richard's youthful story
from nineteen eight to nineteen twelve,
the Petersburg Conservatory,
was in the hands of Glazunov,
composer and administrator,
who made its reputation greater,
increasing opportunities
for Jewish child prodigies.
Since many of them came to Auer,
my Richard got to know quite well
Poliakin, Piastro, and Seidél,
then Heifetz, genius of the hour,
the 'old professor's' pride and joy,
the Silver Age's golden boy.

X.

Although with jewels the age was rife, its
unlikely you will ever find
a more bedazzling one than Heifetz -
he truly was one of a kind.
But from the boyish superhero
I turn now to my youthful hero,
about to enter Petrograd,
chemú byl chrezvychájno rad.[1]
For Richard Petrograd was truly
a turning point in many ways;
at first he wandered in a daze,
as similar to any newly-
arrived, before his eyes unfurled
"a completely different world."[2]

---

[1] *chemu byl* [. . .] = about which he was very glad (Russian).
[2] Richard Burgin (Dann tapes).

XI.

And Richard was "a different person,"
who had rethought and changed his goal;
perhaps New York had put a curse on
the super-virtuoso role;
perhaps his nerves just couldn't take it,
perhaps he feared he wouldn't make it,
and reconsidering his worth,
resolved that an orchestral berth
would suit him and his talent better;
perhaps his overreaching sought
relief from being overwrought;
perhaps he felt he was a debtor,
and hated leaving unrepaid
the sacrifice his father made.

XII.

But anyway, my hero, giving
much thought to future and to fame,
decided that to earn a living
would henceforth be his primary aim.
He'd strive to be a good musician
and hope a permanent position
would ultimately come his way,
so he could settle down one day.
And thus, he took the course pragmatic,
or as he called it, "practical":
he shunned the theoretical,
reversed the order axiomatic,
that might describe his early start,
and put the horse *before* the cart.

XIII.

Perhaps you find this unromantic,
or too mundanely true-to-life,
and you had visions of a frantic,
exceptional youth of storm and strife.
It's true the disciplined and stoic
may not evoke the mode heroic,
and readers may prefer, of course,
a stallion to a good work horse;
but we can't all be lion tamers,
defenders of the barricades,
heroes of the Light Brigades,
impassioned and quixotic gamers.
It's hard to live your life with dash,
unless you have some extra cash.

XIV.

As Byron noted, what's exciting
about perpetual poverty?
or quintessentially indicting
about well-earned security?
I too have learned that annual earnings
can help fulfill *some* inner yearnings,

....
....
....
....
....
....
....
....

XV.
So Richard's worries over money
I understand entirely;
his passing up the milk and honey
of fame, though, still amazes me.
When in my youth applause seemed manna
I'd never get, he'd say, 'Diana,
my darling girl, why do you cry?
It's unimportant, *really*...I
hate seeing you so pessimistic!'
And soothing his discomfiture,
he'd add, 'I think you're too mature
for this, and being unrealistic.'
'You say that,' I'd retort, 'because
you have always heard applause!'

XVI.
I even thought he might be lying.
I now don't think so, but, as then,
his answer isn't satisfying,
although I do know why and when
his feelings underwent revision,
resulting in his proud decision
to view fame with insouciance
as ''something of no consequence.''
It helps to know his self-effacement,
and widely-noted modesty,
were ultimately traits which he
developed, struggling, in replacement
for far less saintly ones inside:
pure arrogance and stubborn pride.

XVII.

And so it was in Peter's *górod*[1]
where stark ambivalencies surged,
through winters frigid, summers torrid,
that Richard's double self emerged:
a dreamer of his dreaming leery,
a theorist debunking theory,
an artist cynical of art,
a reasoning and passionate heart,
a man of peace, in talk contentious,
a dogmatist and diplomat,
who could concede while standing pat,
a great pretender unpretentious,
who in the view of everyone
was flattering, but fawned on none.

XVIII.

But that's enough dichotomizing
of Richard's character in youth,
or I shall risk lobotomizing
with slashes, complicated truth.
Besides, I really have neglected
to give those facts, which you expected,
about his teacher, friends, routine,
and the Conservatory scene;
I've overlooked the circumstantial,
waxed on in generalities,
intuited antimonies,
which factually are insubstantial;
and so I think it would be meet
to turn to matters more concrete.

---

[1] *gorod* = city (Russian)

XIX.

Let's start with Auer. He came to Russia
as concertmaster for the Ballet,
had learned the violin in Prussia
and was Joachim's prodigé.
He made his reputation teaching
in Petersburg, forever preaching
the virtue of strict discipline
for mastering the violin:
"Auer always put importance
on diligence, assiduousness,
hard work, and conscientiousness;
he stressed appearance, health, endurance,
and twenty as the cut-off age
for big careers on the stage."[1]

XX.

These words about Professor Auer
are from a monograph I read,
by Raaben, Lev—a Soviet scholar;
they echo others in my head,
which I shall versify verbatim
(in part at least), and seriatim,
as Burgin, then an older man,
recalled his studies to Mr. Dann
for tape-recorded reproduction.
"It was the opposite, you see,
from Lotto's way, and new to me.
With Auer, that was *class* instruction.
You each played individually,
in class, which meant that usually,

---

[1] Quoted from Lev Raaben, *Leopold Auer*, Moscow, 1962. Original in Russia, translation mine [DLB].

XXI.

"you could, at *most*, spend twenty minutes
to play whatever you'd prepared;
and everybody else was present -
to skip a class, few people dared.
Not that it was obligatory,
but custom at the Conservatory,
since what was really interesting
and valuable was *listening*
to one another at the lesson.
That's how we *learned*, and in my view,
my colleagues had much more to do
with what I learned than the professor.
But listening *was* a useful tool
provided by the Auer school.

XXII.

"Also, I must give him credit
especially for one other thing -
his great respect for the printed letter;
the letter—it meant everything!
You didn't dare to change the letter
of the composer, 'who knew better
than you,' he'd say 'what should be heard,'
and that was in the printed word.
But it is helpful to a student
to discipline himself, you see,
and learn to have respect, when he
is young, professionally unproven.
Ja! discipline was Auer's way,
and a great asset, I must say.

XXIII.

"The rest, however, was a question
of each one playing pretty much
the same as others. He made suggestions,
but didn't really teach as such.
Of course, it's hard to be objective;
you have a different perspective,
when you are actually studying,
than later when considering. . .
You don't know, really, which conception
is truer, since you're influenced by
your own ideas, and time, so I
should say it is my own perception,
the only place where I could see
that Auer showed his artistry

XXIV.

"was chamber music class, his passion.
Ja, he was wonderful in quartet!
although, at times, as was his fashion,
he could get terribly upset.
His rages really were dismaying -
once, I remember, we were playing
Beethóven,[1] Opus Fifty Nine,
and everything was going fine.
We played, he stood there, made no comment,
just listened, utterly absorbed,
you know, and looking at the score;
and at this very touching moment,
I play these insignificant -
or so I thought—embellishments,

---

[1] As a native speaker of Russian, Burgin often stressed Beethoven's name on the second syllable.

XXV.

"when suddenly, his voice, like thunder,
roars at me, 'You carpenter!'[1]
like hitting you in back. In wonder
I looked, as if 'What is it, sir?!
What's wrong?' Then thunderous words came, saying,
'*Do you know what you are playing?!*
Those grace notes, carpenter, are *tears*!
Those are *tears*! He's crying here!'...
He saw a picture, a situation,
a feeling of emotions there...
but chamber music, that was where
he really gives you education;
you felt you had an artist, though
he could get very mean, you know.

XXVI.

"In fact, one time, when giving vent to
his fury at my colleague, in
quartet, he threw the score, and meant to
hit him, but hit his violin;
and that entailed a very major
repair, and all because he raged at
some little thing, from his perspective, absolutely incorrect."

....
....
....
....
....
....

---

[1] "Carpenter, in Russian, is the worst thing you can be. I mean, that's the lowest you can go, when you can only cut wood, you know. It's like in German, *Schuster*, you know, although Hans Sachs was one. That's the lowest you can get in profession." (Richard Burgin, Dann Tapes.)

XXVII.

Since Burgin had the chance to áir his
opinions on his violin
professor, it is only fairness
to give his teacher's views of him.
Of these I have two indications:
remarks on his examinations
(which Raaben mentions), and a note
from Auer to Moisey, I quote:
"I'm pleased to say your son is truly
working very well, and he,
both musically and technically,
is one of my best pupils. Only,
his violin is underpar,
which could his solo career mar."[1]

XXVIII.

His comment on the examinations,
as Raaben indicates, reflects
"his often terse evaluations:
'plays very well in all respects.' "
I'd say, in sum, B-plus/A-minus,
which my hero felt was fine, as
he worried less what grade he made,
than whether he would make the grade.
For him the pressure came from keeping
his promise to repay in kind
the debt that preyed upon his mind
and sometimes hindered him from sleeping:
his father had made Richard's bed
not so he'd sleep, but get ahead.

---

[1] Letter from Auer to M. Burgin, February 23, 1911. Original in Russian.

XXIX.

To Richard that meant education
be utilized efficiently
as academic preparation
for practical activity.
Thus, what he learned in winter classes,
he played in summer for the masses
at music festivals, to earn
the money necessry to learn.
He played in Kharkov, Kiev, Riga,
gained valuable experience,
met people of some influence,
whom he impressed as able, eager,
appreciative of work and tips
on future concertmasterships.

XXX.

Since Richard saw no contradiction
between his schooling and his life,
he did not suffer that affliction
with which *my* younger years were rife.
An alien to alienation,
who could not stomach separation,
his motto was—participate,
assimilate, and integrate;
his goal in life was harmonizing,
and that is why he made the choice
to play his fiddle, single-voiced,
in concert, not in concertizing;
for group endeavor was the form
in which he would exceed the norm.

XXXI.

In groups he shone as mediator
of other people's little rifts,
and in his own right as debater
of rather formidable gifts.
The rule which guided his behavior,
in many arguments the savior,
the apogee of *comme il faut*,
was—always being in the know.
Like many bright young men in college,
intolerant of stupidity,
and fearing most naivety,
he put a premium on knowledge,
and was respected by his peers,
as quite experienced for his years.

XXXII.

His main experience over others
was all the travelling he had done,
and to his more provincial brothers
he seemed most cosmopolitan.
He had a knack for storytelling,
spun a witty yarn as well in
his native Russian as *auf Deutsch*,
and even knew some English *voits*.
In groups he often was the speaker,
but knew enough to listen too,
in conversation one of few,
who used the force of being meeker;
he could defer, did not get sore,
and so, he never was a bore.

XXXIII.

In youth he had in his possession
a quality he never lost,
for which our language lacks expression,
but Russians call, *obshchitelnost*.
The usual one-word translation
does not convey its combination
of joyous sociability
and fervent communality.
Yet, as a youth, his democratic
enjoyment of community,
and preaching of equality,
revealed a source aristocratic:
as noble Excellence's liege,
he exercised *noblesse oblige*.

XXXIV.

Or as he put it, he was "cocky,"
believed himself to be mature,
allowed occasional self-mockery,
without becoming insecure.
He could take lighthearted teasing,
but he would rarely tease, since pleasing
others, was his primary need;
yet he would not cajole or plead.
The thing he took the greatest pride in
was, even if taken down a peg,
he never ever stooped to beg;
but here, dear reader, he was riding
for a fall, since the above
held true until. . .he fell in love.

XXXV.

How many kinds of love we suffer!
But I'm convinced by far the worst,
in terms of being pride's rebuffer,
has got to be the one called 'first.'
Our hearts are never more afire
in red-hot ovens of desire;
we never more perversely shove
our egos in, than in first love;
and never shall another passion
drain the color from our cheeks,
or orphan us for weeks and weeks,
like arson victims, faces ashen,
in shock, deprived of any sense,
and naked in our innocence.

XXXVI.

For us and all the world to ponder,
first love flays vanity alive,
and stings our egos so, we wonder
if we'll our searing wounds survive,
or just remain a mass of squealing,
raw, exacerbated feeling,
whose lips occasionally spurt
one pained refrain, 'I'm hurt!, I'm hurt!'
Against first love we've no defenses:
it sickens, often breaks our hearts,
torments some other body parts,
and crowning all of these offenses,
no other kind of love can be
so lacking in equality.

XXXVII.

F. Tiutchev,* in "Predestination,"
affirms the inequality
of hearts "in fateful combination" -
the softer dies, inevitably.
Although he writes of all romances,
we cannot help but know the chances
of being tossed a fatal glove
are greater when we're first in love.
Turgenev, in his poignant story,
reveals how youthful love does in
the hero and the heroine
through destinies non-amatory:
he loves her and defers therefore,
to him she loves, a predator.

XXXVIII.

And what about the virgin Myshkin?
(I know I've used this rhyme before,
but for my proof, I'll take the risk in
recalling him to you once more.)
He loves Nastasya,* but won't wróng her
so she prefers his rival stronger,
and hates him, since his love is pure,
and her 'first love' has ruined her.
O victims of first love! Nastasya,
Tatiana,* Lensky,* Anna K.,
Natasha,* Sonia, Prince Andrey,*
Bazarov, Mary, Bèla, Asya* -
your sufferings are everywhere,
convincing us first love's unfair.

XXXIX.

There is a method in the madness
of this digressionary tract;
for me my hero's love and sadness
is mostly fantasy, not fact.
Although I hate to be untruthful,
what can I do? For Richard's youthful
romance I have no real-life source,
no memoirs, and must needs recourse
to books I know, and pure invention.
And since the one fact I did get,
his first love's first name, Henriette,
in what I'll tell, it's my intention
to shield my lovers' innocence
behind fictitious incidents.

XL.

Perhaps not totally fictitious,
but based upon my own surmise;
I do not want to be capricious,
yet oftentimes it seems unwise
to say what is true information
and what is real imagination.
Of what transpires in my plot,
some things happened, some did not,
but it's not spurious, rather *my* sense
of truth despite reality;
at times, you know, I must be free
to exercise poetic license,
since I'm the artist of my *Life*,
and Richard Burgin's after-life.

XLI.

"In anything there should be freedom,
and more than anywhere in art,
but there's a point where this can't *bé* done -
when you exaggerate your part,
you lose all sense of the proportions,
and freedom then becomes distortion.
As Goethe put it—*und bestimmt!* -
'*Man reckt der Absicht, und wird verstimmt.*'"[1]
The quoter of this thought shall guide me:
my story I shall freely tell,
but try to stay in tune as well.
(Who is he? Reader, don't deride me
if I don't say, for I confess
I think you probably can guess.)

---

[1] "One stretches the intention and feels out of tune."

CHAPTER FOUR: FIRST LOVE

And then SHE would appear
- Tolstoy

Oh, she no doubt will answer,
And, maybe, she will kiss -

- Akhmatova

I. II. III.
IV.

The more I knew about my hero,
the easier I made things up,
more thirstily drank down to zero,
the spirits of my muse's cup.
Intoxicated with deceiving,
and biographical word-weaving,
we spun my hero's yarn till youth
to suit our pleasure, not the truth;
but our strange quasi-life-based diction,
blown up like Epiphánii's* Lives,
unfortunately only thrives
on facts inflatable with fiction,
and now, deprived of her balloon,
my muse has fallen in a swoon.

V.

How tedious to lack invention
and start to write a stanza out
without belief in your pretension
to knowing what you'll write about;
how dull to check infertile rages
by crumpling up the half-filled pages
which failed at telling what, if told,
would doubtless leave your readers cold;
how tiresome the self-reproachings,
the hopes, and vows, and timid dreams,
the crossed-out lines, rejected themes,
and stop-gap literary poachings;
the imagination overtaxed
by glaring paucities of facts.

VI.

This was my Slavist's situation,
when starting her romantic tale;
she called her muse for inspiration,
but saw she looked distinctly pale.
By résearch data clearly spoiled,
her muse instinctively recoiled,
in horror at the mere surmise,
that she would have to improvise;
but still she tried. For days she mumbled
the same three stanzas fifty times,
with trite or simply missing rhymes,
rhythm jagged, syntax jumbled,
until, about to lose her wits,
my Slavist cried, 'Let's call it quits!

VII.

'Enough of futile versifying,
my darling muse! We'll work instead
on something far more gratifying
to you, who have been born and bred
on modes and musings academic.'
'Your flattery is stratagemic,'
her muse replied, 'but for this breach
I owe you. Where's your Tolstoy speech?'
Thus *Richard Burgin* was forgotten
for "Death and Women in Tolstoy:
A Jungian View." My Slavist's ploy
was happily not misbegotten.
Tolstoy revived her muse's breath,
and thus has saved my *Life* from death.

VIII.

But now that we have finally started
on chapter four, left three behind,
and have tetrameterly charted
the in-between, we must rewind
our reel a bit to our depiction
of Richard when first love's affliction
infected him, and this, we glean,
befell him when he was sixteen.
So, reader, now we're off together
to early summer, nineteen ten;
my hero was in Pávlovsk* then,
relaxing in the straw-hat weather,
a carefree youth, until he met
a fellow student, Henriette.

IX.

A lovely day! I hear the trolling
of birds and strings in summer air,
and there I see my Richard strolling
the wooded path, without a care;
but now he stops and starts to listen,
smiles, and his eyes aglisten,
he murmurs, 'Sure, I know that sound,
the *Kreutzer*,...but?' he looks around,
'but isn't that a *piano* playing
the part that Lotto played with me
on violin?! How can this be?'
He runs to see without delaying,
and syncopates his gait with grins,
'I'd swear 'twas for two violins!'[1]

---

[1] "You know, when I first got acquainted with the *Kreutzer Sonata* I knew it as a piece for two violins because my teacher, Lotto, he played everything, all accompaniments, on the violin. And the first time I heard that with a piano was during the summer, out of town. I was in the country and there was some young violinist and a pianist who practiced there, and I happened to come in, when I heard the music, you know—and it impressed me enormously, because I was crazy about that piece. Even for two violinists, I was crazy about it. It was a new world." (Richard Burgin)

X.

He finds the *dácha*, knocks, all flushing.
'Why Richard! What a nice surprise!'
'Borís! Oh please forgive my rushing
in, but. . .' 'Don't apologize.
Come in, come in. We're only playing
for fun. But tell me, where're you staying?'
'Nearby. I thought that I'd explore
a bit, and heard you. I adore
that piece, but thought, was I naive!, it,'
he blushed, 'it's, well, the first I heard
it played with, isn't this absurd?!,
with *piano*!' 'No, I can't believe it!
You're joking.' 'Yes, it's true, I swear,
so when I heard a piano there,

XI.

'I thought,' he turned to Borya's pianist,
'I don't believe we've ever met?'
'Now I'm the one who's lacking manners,'
laughed Borya, 'Richard—Henriette,
Benois-Èfron's* most gifted student!'
She smiled, 'Borya, that's imprudent,
suppose I can't live up to it?'
'Oh, I don't think you've got a bit
to worry. . .' Richard interjected,
'what I heard you played beautifully.
I'm pleased to meet you.' 'Same for me.'
A pause. Their smiles intersected;
then Richard, gazing in her eyes,
said, 'Borya's praise was very wise.'

XII.

He blushed and thought, 'Oh that was worthy
of some banál Lothario,
she probably thinks I'm pretty nervy,
or awfully young. I'd better go.'
But his resolve was soon forgotten,
when Borya said, 'It's getting hot and
I'm as hungry as a horse!
So let's eat! You'll stay of course?'
'I'd love to but. . .' 'No "buts" accepted,
I hate them, like apologies.'
He stayed; they lunched on rolls and cheese,
and talked, while Borya intercepted
a glance or two that we'd call vibes,
but graciously refrained from jibes.

XIII.

Perhaps, dear reader, you are curious,
not just about this Henriette,
but also Richard's comrade, Bóris.
They played together in quartet,
had met through Mischa, Borya's brother,
and from the start they liked each other,
and found some common interests
in chamber music, bridge, and chess.
However, Borya, somewhat older,
and in some ways more worldly-wise,
occasionally would patronize.
This made my youthful Richard smoulder,
but pride, of course, forbade him bend
enough to say, 'Don't condescend.'

XIV.

Boris knew this, and tried to curb his
need to play the despotist,
but seeing Henriette disturb his
friend, he just could not resist.
Next day, he said, as they were leaving
rehearsal, 'Could it be you're grieving?
or sick? To look at you, you'd think
last night you hadn't slept a wink!
She must have made a BIG impression!'
But Richard wouldn't be enticed,
and simply smiled, 'Yes, she's nice.'
'Just nice? Come on, your pale expression
says otherwise. Why, Lord above,
admit it, brother, you're in love!'

XV.

'Oh, Borya, stop! I've seen her once and
so what? It's stupid making such
a fuss, I...' 'Richard, I'm no dunce and
methinks this man protests too much!'
'I'm not protesting, only saying,
I liked her, and admired her playing,
and that is all, there's nothing more.'
'So when've you looked like this before?'
And reader, that was the beginning.
Though Richard managed to escape
from Borya's taunts without a scrape,
the features he had found so winning
tormented him again that night,
and made him realize, 'Borya's right.'

XVI.

Indeed, it's true, my hero's smitten;
I don't know if that's good or bad,
or both; the theme's been overwritten,
there's very little I can add.
I've said that fun is in the doing;
perhaps undoing's in the wooing:
in love, when all's undone, unsaid,
you feel you might as well be dead,
or failing that, there's always sleeping;
in sleep alone can love be fair,
for dreams knit lovers' sleeves of care
so well, that waking leaves them weeping.
The more impossible love seems,
the more realizable in dreams.

XVII.

So Richard spent his nights that summer
in high-fidelity reveries,
while friends remarked upon his dumber,
and very strange (for him) unease
at social gatherings, whenever
a "certain girl" was there; however,
they had no inkling how he shone
in dream-talk home, with HER alone.
For all the social decrescendos
that left my Richard's tongue so tied
would build again when it was plied
by HER to deafening crescendos,
which climaxed, drowning out real life,
when SHE in dreams became his wife.

XVIII.

But who's this object of desire?
Who is Sylvia? What is she?
The light of Richard's youthful fire
remains quite in the dark for me.
I've not, like Solomon,* uncovered
the mystery of this great beloved;
I've only found elusive clues,
and hence, her portrait's dusky hues:
her origins were Polish-Jewish;
she was a Silver Laureate,
in nineteen ten a graduate,
a beauty (some say, cold and shrewish),
intense, a bit imperious,
intelligent, and virtuous.

XIX.

She was also probably older
than Richard, by a couple years.
Perhaps that's why he wasn't bolder,
and had so many boyish fears.
An older woman's fascinating,
but surely it was devastating
to sense the more he sang her praise,
the more he sang his youthful ways;
but by her age he was attracted,
and by her beauty, talent, taste;
yet 'twas her virtue that laid waste
his heart in agony protracted;
for what enticement can there be
more virulent than purity?

XX.

I'll skip a lengthy dissertation
in praise of Virtue's attitude;
for me it lacks all titillation,
and I'm a wanderlusty prude;
I merely note, 'twas not the siren
who ultimately caught Lord Byron -
he sacrificed the lissome Lamb*
for Princess Parallelogram* -
and also bring to your attention
the very captivating hold
on Richard's peer-group of the old
Tolstoy, who wisely preached prevention
against the *Kreutzer's* provenance
of sinister concupiscence.

XXI.

Like others, Richard venerated
the Yasnian-Polianian sage;
it seemed his thought encapsulated
the highest strivings of their age.
His aspiration to perfection,
the ethics of his bold rejection
of false authorities for TRUTH
inspired idealistic youth;
but there was something in addition
that drew my Richard to Tolstoy
and made the seer seem *rodnóy*,[1]
a vague, but deepheld supposition,
that Tólstoy felt since childhood,
like him, a sense of orphanhood.

---

[1] *rodnóy* = near-and-dear; native (Russian)

XXII.

Though Richard's parents still were living,
he felt detached, as if in Rome,
completely romanized, yet giving
himself the lie that it was home.
And where was home? and "where was mother?"[1]
He felt, before they'd known each other,
he'd been "ejected from the nest"
with the injunction: do your best!
He missed her very much, and worried
about her health. He'd dream at night
how he could still make things all right
for her, before she. . .if he hurried
back home to her; then SHE would get
somehow confused with. . .Henriette.

XXIII.

Thus summer dreams passed into autumn
realities and sad good-byes,
and Richard, waking up, hit bottom
the day of parting, with tearful eyes,
for Henriette was off to Poland,
and Richard, feeling very low and
convinced his destiny was cruel,
would soon be going back to school;
but he resolved that his behavior
at the station would not betray
a trace of sadness or dismay;
he wiped his tears, and pride, his savior,
rebuked him, saying, 'Don't give in!
You've got to have some discipline.'

---

[1] Quotations from Tolstoy's *Confession*.

XXIV.

He went with Bóris to the station
and joined the muted, milling throng's
mixed chorus cadencing vacation
in whispered codas of so longs;
but just before the final, killing
farewell, he heard one alto trilling
above his *ppp 'Proshcháj!'*[1]
'Oh I'll be back, it's not good-bye.'
An unforeseen appoggiatura
had lightly graced his parting note,
and brought a lump to Richard's throat,
but also made him feel securer,
that with this movement's loss of heart,
a more enlivening one would start.

XXV.

But when? And how? All September,
as respite from the daily grind,
he'd fall to musing, and remember
her parting words to try and find
what kind of future they might presage:
had they contained a silent message,
that she'd be back to be with him?
or were the chances of that slim?
And so he plucked his mental daisy
of joyous/gloomy shifts in thought,
'She likes me,/No, she likes me not,'
until what really drove him crazy
was not the yesses or the no's,
but his concluding I-don't-know's.

---

[1] *Proshcháj* = farewell (Russian).

XXVI.

At last he realized this not knowing
the way she felt was "killing" him,
and sensed determination growing -
you know the kind, we call it "grim" -
to make some sort of, well, confession,
that would elicit an expression
from HER, of how SHE felt about
the man her feelings left in doubt
so cruel, rejection would be better.
But should he risk it face-to-face?
No, that could mean complete disgrace;
but if?...yes, if he...wrote a letter?!
'Why that,' he grinned, 'would save the day!
For once I'm glad that she's away.'

RICHARD'S LETTER TO HENRIETTE[1]

11.X.10
      Dear Henriette!
I'm writing you—don't be offended!
For what could cause me more regret?
I know, however you pretended,
you have the right to be upset,
but you, since you have condescended
to be my friend, will understand
that I must do my heart's command.
At first I did not think of writing;
believe me: had I kept my pride,
you would have had no cause to chide,
or known the battle I've been fighting.
Yet, the more I fight, the more I find
I just can't get you off my mind.

---

[1] Richard's letter to Henrietta adheres to the rhyme pattern and structure of Tatiana's letter to Onegin in Pushkin's *Eugene Onegin.*

Oh if, that morning at the station,
you'd only let your words reveal
more clearly how you really feel,
I might have stood our separation.
But what you said spawned endless doubt,
and so, I'm forced to write this letter
to tell you how I feel, straight out.
I miss, and love you, Henrietta.

I wonder if I wasn't cursed
by overhearing that Sonata?
You took my breath away at first,
and I've been holding it *fermata*
until this banal *serenata*...
Yet this I know—the piano part
was but the least that I recovered,
for when you played it, I discovered
the missing pianist of my heart.

But I have had enough of groping
for words to make my feelings clear.
I now am quite resigned to hoping
for a reply I also fear.
Boris (who often seems my rival)
expects you back in just three weeks -
and what will come with your arrival?
Shall you reject what Richard seeks?
Or will you...? No! the mere suggestion
of such enormous happiness
might in itself subvert success.
Instead of finishing the question,
I think that I prefer to end
my letter in anticipation,

with a collegial invitation,
that I am making as a friend.
The conservatory's dedicating
a chamber concert to Fauré,
and our quartet's participating.
There's no way of exaggerating
my joy if you could hear us play,
in fact, we all would be delighted!
In any case, you are invited -
November, the 13th, at two.
Boróvsky's playing pianoforte -
Vtoróy kvartét,[1] a pleasant sort, he
plays well, but not so well as you.
Please come.

    And so, my Henrietta,
I'll close now, hoping that my letter
won't strike you as too "out of tune."
Forgive me if it sounded sappy.
I hope we'll see each other soon,
and you have been both well and happy.
So all the best,
              I press your hand,
              Your Richard
              (in the "fatherland")

---

[1] *Vtoróy kvartét* = Second Quartet (Russian). The piece in question is Fauré's Second Quartet for Pianoforte, Violin, Viola, and Cello in g minor, Op. 45.

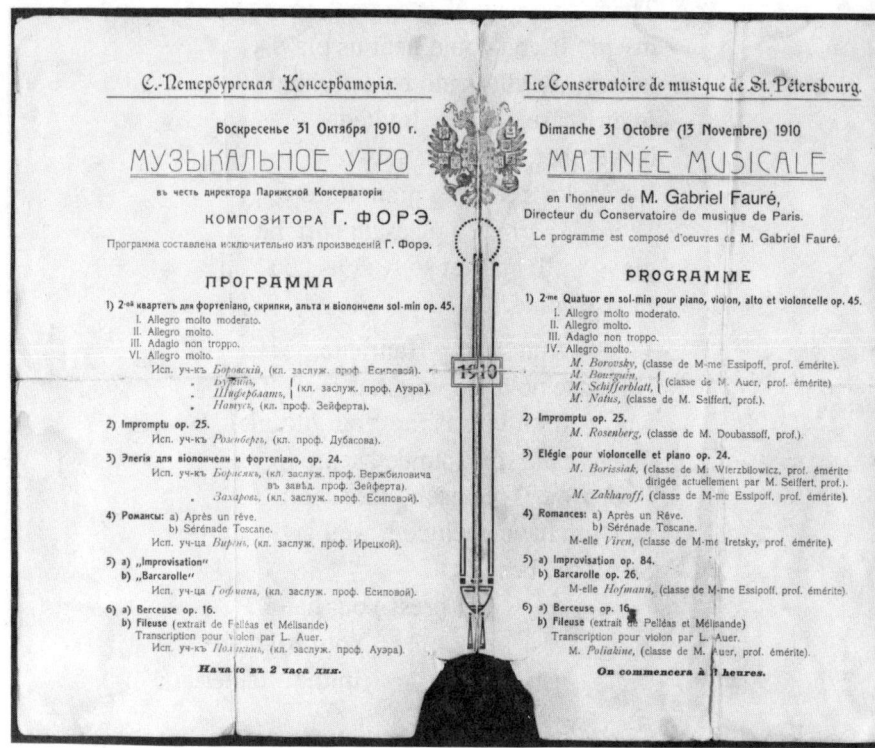

Program of the "Musical Matinee" in honor of Gabriel Fauré, given at the St. Petersburg Conservatory of Music on October 31 (old style), 1910. Richard performed in the quartet which opens the program.

XXVII. XXVIII. XXIX.

I've learned a lack of expectations -
the question 'Will s/he?,' answer, 'Nope!' -
is one of those expostulations
with which we mask a wealth of hope.
The poorer our predicted pleasure,
the richer are the hopes we treasure;
the more we say 'Impossible!'
the more we pray it's possible.
Thus Richard, having sent his letter,
would tell himself each morning, 'I
am certain she will not reply,
and in a way that's probably better.'
Yet through the mail-less days and nights
he mutely prayed, 'I hope she writes.'

XXX.

Alas, dear reader, as expected
in situations of no hope,
she didn't write. Although dejected,
my Richard tried his best to cope
with unacknowledged disappointment.
He soothed himself with work, an ointment
that may provide the sole relief
for disappointed lovers' grief.
He plunged into quartet rehearsals,
eagerly prepared for class,
refused to think about the lass
responsible for the reversals
in hopes he now could not ignore,
although they made his ego sore.

XXXI.

Time fairly flew. Before he knew it,
the concert day was drawing nigh;
and while to friends he would pooh-pooh it,
inside, his hopes were riding high.
His overworked imagination,
or what we'd call pure compensation,
had led my Richard to opine
her silence was a hopeful sign.
'If I were she,' he thought, 'I'd write me,
if what I'd say would make me sad,
but if I knew 'twould make me glad,
I'd want in person to delight me.
The concert's surely my trump card!'
(O Lord, do youthful hopes die hard!)

XXXII.

The thirteenth. Rising in a hurry,
my Richard washed with special care,
and dressed amid a furious flurry,
though having but one suit to wear.
He rubbed the spots out, brushed it speckless,
blacked his shoes and shone them fleckless,
till even the soles were free of dirt,
put on (of four) his least-worn shirt,
attached his newest, crispest collar,
checked out his tie ('Thank God, no spot!')
and fumbling for the perfect knot,
he heard his cousin (room-mate) holler,
'Hey Richard! We have got to go!
It's almost one o'clock, you know!'

XXXIII.

Expecting well-deserved berating,
he runs backstage, and out of breath,
he greets his colleagues, clustered, waiting,
their faces anxious, pale as death.
'At last!' they gasp. 'Thank God, what worry
you've caused!' 'I know, I'm awfully sorry,
I. . .' 'Never mind, at least you're here,
and that alone is cause for cheer.'
'No time for talk! Let's go already.'
With serious faces, trembling hands,
they enter, bow, adjust their stands;
then Richard, overcome by heady
excitement, hears Borovsky's *A*,
prepares to start and thinks 'Fauré. . .

XXXIV.

will SHE?. . .' He feels a flash of fright and
steals a look around the hall. . .
Suddenly his pupils brighten,
he smiles, staring and enthralled.
'She's here! She's sitting there, and smiling!
Is there a face that's more beguiling?'
He concentrates his gaze ahead,
straight at her, and. . .she nods her head.
The concert is for him a mixture
of trying hard to play his best,
and seeking glances when at rest;
four movements pass and paint a picture. . .
and just as from the sonorous mist
he sees emerge a lovers' tryst

XXXV.

backstage, his dreams are interrupted!
No more of passionate pretend;
with loud applause the hall's erupted;
amazed that they have reached the end,
he seeks her eyes. Their sideways motion
directs his exit, through commotion
backstage, and pushing through the door,
he bursts into the corridor.
She waves her hand, ('Should I kiss it?')
Instead his lips move to exclaim,
'Oh, Henriette, I'm glad you came!'
'Richard! Did you think I'd miss it?'
'Well. . .' 'Silly! but. . . let's take a walk.
It's noisy here, and we. . .must talk.'

XXXVI.

Ah, walks and talks! I'm sure, dear reader,
like me, you've had your share of them,
both those when you're the verbal leader,
and those in which you haw and hem.
They range from arias sweet and charming,
to portents dire and alarming:
some walks and talks exhilirate,
while other ones exasperate,
and like their moods, their tempo markings
can vary, from *andante* strolls,
to rigid, *à la marche* patrols,
from *largo* drags to *allegro* larkings,
and there are polyrythmic ones
with syncopations, rests, and runs.

XXXVII.

Some depend upon the setting,
as much as on your general mood;
some environs can be upsetting,
while others make you feel quite good.
It's hard to pinpoint interactions
between the place and one's reactions;
does Nature feel our souls' dismay,
or does she make us feel that way?
The question's mooter if a city
is where you walk. It seems to be,
or have, a personality,
that's capable of hate and pity,
and oftentimes exerts a force
upon its walkers' future course.

XXXVIII.

Of this perhaps the prime example
occurs in Russian literature;
a most unscientific sample
of texts on Petersburg's allure -
so potently sublime, horrific,
irrational and scientific -
reveals how much that city's streets
control successes and defeats
of walkers: Dostoevsky's heroes,
the generous dreamers and the mean,
Pushkin's Hermann* and Eugene,*
and numerous Gogolian* zeroes -
in every case the city stalks,
and orchestrates their walks and talks.

XXXIX.

Its snowy-wet November weather
infects them, chills them to the bone;
in June white nights they come together,
or stroll the desolate quays alone;
its flooding Néva drives them crazy,
its labyrinthe traps brilliant, lazy
Raskolnikov[1] to dream of crimes;
its monuments inspire rhymes;
its streetlamps, lighted by the Devil,[2]
create illusions of pure love,
or mournful shadows of the Dove;[3]
its youthful dreamers weep and revel;
and its broad prospects were the set
of Richard's talk from Henriette.

---

[1] Raskolnikov, the hero of Dostoevsky's *Crime and Punishment*.
[2] In "Nevsky Prospect" Gogol comments, "The Devil lights the streetlamps on Nevsky Prospect, making everything appear not in its true light." The illusionary quality of the city leads the two heroes of this story to pursue beautiful women, who turn out to be not at all what they seem.
[3] In Andrey Bely's *Petersburg*, the streets of the city are haunted by a shadowy, luminous figure, suggestive of Christ.

XL.

It started as is customary:
'I hope you had a pleasant trip?'
'Yes, very nice, if ordinary.
And you? How goes the studentship,
[he winced], I mean, conservatory?'
'Oh, nothing new, the usual story;
it seems right now we only talk
about Tolstoy...'[1] 'Yes, what a shock!'
'It made me sad, but now I'm better,
I guess because...because you're back,
and I...but, now I'm on this track,'
he paused, 'well, did you get my letter?'
'I did.' 'You didn't answer, why?'
'I'd rather... talk.' She heaved a sigh.

XLI.[2]

'I read, reread, your every word and
I loved you ... for your honesty,
and yet, it also was a burden,
since you deserve the same from me.
To say this really isn't easy -
I'm even feeling sort of queasy -
but, well, I...like you, quite a lot,
I do, but, frankly, love it's not.
And now, I guess, I mostly worry
that you'll not only be upset,
but think I'm playing the coquette,
so please believe I'm truly sorry,
that you and I don't feel the same,
but, really, I am not to blame.

---

[1] Tolstoy died on November 7, 1910.
[2] Just as Tatiana's letter to Onegin served as the model for Richard's to Henriette, so Onegin's verbal response to her (in chapter IV) provides the model for Henriette's "talk" with Richard.

XLII.

'I've just not known yet that sensation,
that kind of. . .love, which you avow,
but if it's any consolation -
though probably it won't be now -
if my heart were set afire
with love, and yearning, and. . .desire,
I couldn't find, I swear it's true,
a better man to love than you;
and though I do not feel the passion
which you must feel, and who knows why?
to say I'm cold would be a lie,
for I do love you, in my fashion,
not as a lover—why pretend? -
but as a sister and a friend.

XLIII.

'I do not want to make you suffer,
but I have something else to say,
that I'm afraid might make it tougher
for you to cope with your dismay,
and put more strain on our relations
as colleagues here. Since graduation
I've had to think, as you must know,
about my plans, and where I'll go.
Well, I've accepted an appointment
from Auer, to accompany. . .
we'll be together frequently,
and I just hope your disappointment
will not prevent, or interfere
with our continued friendship here.'

XLIV.

With that, my Henriette concluded.
They walked in silence till they reached
her lodgings. Richard then exuded
a mournful sigh; his eyes beseeched,
but all his pleas remained unuttered.
He took her hand, with effort muttered
a faint 'so long,' then turned, and left,
trod home funereally, grave, bereft.
He'd never felt more hurt, dejected,
more tired, more disposed to brood,
or in a more self-pitying mood;
'I guess,' he moaned, 'I've been rejected,
a man of sorrows, and in brief,
not unacquainted now with grief.'

XLV.

But don't be sad. Though unrequited
and unfulfilled his love and dream;
unrealized all his hopes, unplighted
his troth, unmanned his self-esteem;
though unconsoled beyond all question,
unmollified by the suggestion,
that's meant to calm, but most offends
rejected lovers, 'let's be friends,'
my hero has not long to languish,
for there's resiliency in youth,
and first love illustrates a truth,
which gives a purpose to its anguish:
one has to drink its bitter cup
way down in order to come up.

CHAPTER FIVE: THE FINNISH CONNECTION

> *And paley dove-gray-bluish eyes*
> *Similar to Finnish skies.*
> *- Baratynsky*

I.

A year went by, nineteen eleven,
and Richard spent it rather well;
his life was hardly seventh heaven,
but neither had it been the hell,
predicted by the black depression,
which followed Henriette's confession
of friendly feelings she was sure
would cast a pall on her allure.
But, then, how often our predictions,
our efforts to control our fate,
do not, in fact, anticipate
the unexpected contradictions
which actual living holds in store,
and no one can predict before.

II.

Thus, Henriette feared her appointment
would only make relations worse,
and Richard feared his disappointment
betokened that their love was cursed.
Yet, in the end, their being together
did not exacerbate the weather,
but actually dispelled the gloom
which previously had forecast doom.
At first a certain discomposure
was evident and talk was strained,
but in a while they regained,
because of mutual exposure,
the ease of shared experience,
and overcame their reticence.

III.

The year had also had attractions
in the realm professional,
which counterpointed the distractions
of disengagements personal.
My Richard's life became so busy,
it left him feeling slightly dizzy,
but work's harmonious resonance
drowned out romantic dissonance.
In March, still feeling in the pits, he
received the opportunity
of playing Scriabin's *Symphony
of Fire* under Koussevitzky.*
It was the Petersburg première,
and greatly brightened his despair.

IV.

The summer brought a separation
from Henriette, which made him glum,
but as a kind of reparation,
his job at Riga was a plum:
his solos with the Philharmonic
of Warsaw were a potent tonic,
and though they left him quite fatigued,
they made him feel he had big-leagued,
and gave him little time to ponder
how much he missed his Henriette,
how much his heart could not forget,
and just how much it had grown fonder.
To be so tired one can't think
surpasses not to sleep a wink.

V.

He had returned that fall assuming
they would continue as before,
as friends and colleagues, just resuming
their work together, nothing more;
yet while collegial relations
remained the same, in conversations
her manner seemed more. . .indirect;
on matters where he would expect
straightforwardness, she played the hinter.
At first he hardly was aware
of her far more elusive air,
but as the fall passed into winter,
he sensed there really was a change;
in fact, she acted downright strange.

VI.

Before, she'd never been offended,
but now she often acted hurt;
before, she never had pretended,
but now she openly would flirt.
Where formerly she'd been judicious,
she now at times became capricious,
and would occasionally employ
devices positively coy.
When once she'd been enthusiastic
and joined in group activities,
she now avoided company,
retreated to a life monastic,
and never let the truth be known
why she preferred to be alone.

VII.

One needs but scant sophistication
to realize what these changes show,
but Richard lacked an education
in sentiment, and didn't know.
Her coyness made him feel unsettled,
by her caprices he was nettled
and pushed to pleading self-defense
for things not meant to cause offense.
He found her presence most perturbing,
and wished at times she'd go away,
but if she did, in just one day,
he found her absence more disturbing:
he had no clue to what it meant?!
(Oh, reader, he was innocent.)

VIII.

Thus, not without some consternation,
my Richard greeted nineteen twelve
and looked ahead. His graduation
next May loomed large; he'd better shelve
his personal worries, since despairing
was not conducive to preparing
for his profession's future chores,
his first real job, in Helsingfors.
(My goodness! I forgot to mention
the most important thing of all
last summer brought—a job next fall!
Please forgive my inattention,
I guess it was one of those times
when facts of life eluded rhymes.)

Richard Burgin in St. Petersburg, around the time of his graduation from the Conservatory in 1912.

IX.

But I shall spare you long reflections
on why my memory misfared,
and turn to Burgin's recollections
of nineteen-twelve, when he prepared
to make the imminent transition
to his Helsingfors position.

....
....
....
....
....
....
....
....

X.

"And my philosophy, I remember,
when going to a foreign land,
I wanted to become a member
of that new culture, understand
the language and the literary
traditions; literature was very
important and interesting for me.
I also tended, musically,
perhaps because I'd lived in Prussia
when I was young, you know, Berlin,
to be more cosmopolitan.
I sort of went outside of Russia,
you know, to find composers who
were different from the ones we knew.

XI.

"So when I knew that it was certain
I'd go to Finland, I found out
about Sibelius's Concerto,
which only then I learned about.
I practiced that, and then I brought it
to class. And Auer had never taught it.
Though Tseitlin* played it—that he knew -
for him it was completely new;
and also Sinding, for example -
I brought to class and played his *Third
Concerto*, which no one had heard,
and Auer, since he liked to sample
new music, had respect for me,
that I would bring it in, you see.

XII.

"And also, when I went to Finland,
I learned, not Finnish actually,
but Swedish, since there were in Finland
still Swedish-speaking Finns, you see.
That was the strangest situation -
a city with a population
which was comparatively small,
a hundred fifty thousand in all,
and in a country of three million,
which also isn't very large,
they had two symphony orchestras,
and each one gave a concert season.
No day would pass, in other words,
without a concert in Helsingfors.

XIII.

"Those two orchestras reflected
the country's ethnic rivalries;
the one that Kájanus* directed
had nationalistic tendencies;
the one I was associated
with, Schnéevoigt's* (who was educated
in Germany, although a Finn),
was more inclined towards Berlin.
But due to this great competition,
those special Finnish politics,
Helsinki's music life was rich,
and Finland's musical position
was really way ahead, I'd say,
of any country of its day."

XIV.

I've quoted Burgin's recollections,
his look behind, to look ahead
and show the various connections
to which his education led,
but in the meantime I've left pending
a situation far more rending
than my young violinist's art,
the future of his tortured heart.
So now I'll do my own backtracking,
pick up the still unwoven strand
I dropped with Richard, nothing planned,
uncomprehendingly alacking,
alassing, angered, and upset
about the change in Henriette.

XV.

Her oddities did not diminish,
but just grew odder in the spring,
and Richard saw his future Finnish
as finishing their future thing.
Again, the clouds of disillusion,
annoyance and irresolution
were gathering and seemed to blight
professional horizons bright.
He tried to talk, but met resistance;
whenever he would ask, 'What's wrong?'
she'd say, 'I've got to go, so long,'
and pleading proved of no assistance:
to his, 'Oh please don't make a scene,'
she'd shrug, 'I don't know what you mean?!'

XVI.

And yet, the more she drove him crazy,
the more, it seemed, he found her dear;
the more she left the future hazy,
the more he wished to make it clear.
At last, one night when he was pondering
her oddities, he started wondering,
'What can I do? What should I say?
There simply has to be some way,
some instrument at my disposal,
to solve this problem...Let me see...
perhaps I'll make her...(suddenly,
the answer sounded)...a proposal!
That's it! If she says yes, it's great;
if no, well, still, I'll know my fate.'

XVII.

Dear reader, I shall skip the détails
of his proposing. Why rehash
the sort of banal scene that retails
in Harlequins for petty cash?
He made it after graduation,
and common to the situation,
his eyes expressed both hope and dread,
he mumbled, and his face was red.
She also blushed, demure, elated
to hear him get it out at last,
then sighed and whispered, breathing fast,
her answer, which you have awaited
for thirteen lines, but now must guess:
one word to rhyme my couplet, ---.

XVIII.

Nor will you hear from me effusions
about my lovers' happiness;
with all such blissful, grand illusions
my muse does not have much success.
She finds it telling that for 'happy'
her most convenient rhyme is 'sappy';
it bores her that in English 'kiss,'
so happily harmonizes 'bliss.'
'In Russian, 'kiss' is more amusing,'
she grinned, 'what rhymes with *potselúi*?'
'Well what?' 'You know,' she whispered, '---.'
(Forgive me, reader, for refusing
to write a word so crass and sick,
it makes my conscience feel a prick.)

XIX.

But onward! What's the greatest hurdle
my youthful lovers have to face?
What can make their hot blood curdle
with thoughts of scandal, shame, disgrace?
What wear-and-tear can snap the suture
with which they have sewn up their future?
What worry turns them into wrecks?
Oh no, you're wrong, it isn't sex;
no, please don't think I'm being funny,
it isn't that, nor their rapport,
nor problems of the mundane sort,
like housing, jobs, or even money;
there's something worse than all of these -
their meetings with their families.

XX.

Perhaps you think I'm either joking,
or have completely lost my mind,
or feel the need to be provoking,
because I have an axe to grind;
but you'd be wrong. It's not derangement
which moves me here, nor some estrangement;
so let me take a little space,
and I shall try to make my case.
....
....
....
....
....
....

XXI.

If I weren't right, what child would grovel?
or wish his home another one?
If I weren't right, what kind of novel
was ever written, or begun?
What plays or films would give enjoyment?
How could there be enough employment
for counselors, psychiatrists,
lawyers, priests, or therapists?
If I weren't right, who'd ever bother
to read the works of Sigmund Freud?
and who would ever get annoyed,
or want to fight with his/her mother?
If I weren't right, (now don't get sore)
all life would stop, or be a bore.

XXII.

For all its worrisome detractions,
woes and tensions very real,
one's family still has great attractions,
especially as an ideal
of happiness. Who doesn't pander
to that beguiling propaganda
that there exists, and yours can be
(with luck) the perfect family?
And never is this feeling stronger
than when you're coming home from school;
it seems your absence has been cruel,
it cannot last a moment longer,
you yearn for home, and hence your zeal
to make your visit there ideal.

XXIII.

What's ideal, you ask? That question,
re families and all other things,
quite frankly gives me indigestion,
and clips my muse's soaring wings.
We can't give positive definitions,
but there are contexts and conditions,
where we'll suggest what it is *not*:
it's *not*, in general, what you've got.
In striving, it is *not* desiring
what is impossible to get,
in setting up, it's *not* upset;
in ending, it is *not* expiring;
in blossoming, it's *not* to wilt;
in family life, it is—*not* guilt.

XXIV.

Guilt! Who'll offer me a reason
why every family structure's built,
when no one has committed treason,
on mutual do-not-blame-me silt?
Is there a way of understanding
the permanent self-reprimanding
which tips us from our cradle's tilt,
and tears to bits our comfort's quilt?
Why do our sincere laudations
to families have a guilty lilt?
Why *is* the Golden Rule so gilt
with burnished self-recriminations?
Why, over milk by parents spilt,
do children burst in tears from guilt?

XXV.

Like everyone, my Richard suffered
from guilt, though he was not aware
of this, since early on he'd buffered
himself against its wear-and-tear,
by showing filial devotion,
behavior based upon the notion,
that he could best avoid complaint
by acting out the role of saint.
He'd made his parents' mute injunction
his own: just try to do your best,
indeed, he never let it rest,
and planned his future in conjunction
with what he knew they would expect,
and loved, and showed them great respect.

XXVI.

The only time he could remember,
when he had disappointed them,
was in that bleak, New York November -
for that, he did himself condemn;
but otherwise, his guilty flurries
were hidden in what he called 'worries,'
that he would ever do again
what might cause his parents pain.
He felt withal he'd been successful;
through graduation—knock on wood! -
he had done well, and had been good;
yet lately feelings most distressful
disturbed his generally guiltless state,
whenever he would contemplate

XXVII.

his visit home. In consternation
he tried to find the reason why
from studious self-examination.
At first it yielded no reply:
indeed, what possible abrasion
could scar this happiest occasion
of sharing joys with kin he missed?
His being a Silver Medalist;
the job that he'd begin next season;
and then, the greatest news of all,
his plans to marry in the fall. . .
There seemed to be no earthly reason
why he should be at all upset,
unless. . .unless'twas. . .Henriette!

XXVIII.

Suddenly, the realization,
ablush with guilt, had dawned on him,
that maybe out of sublimation,
embarrassment, or by some whim,
not once, in person, or by letter,
had he mentioned Henrietta;
so it would come as quite a shock,
when he and she, engaged, would walk
into his home. . .O Lord, what terror!
Oh why had he not paved the way
for bringing home his. . .fiancée?
And now that he had seen his error,
the happiness that lay ahead
betokened nothing if not dread.

XXIX.

So, reader, what's your expectation?
Has Richard's guilty prophecy
foreseen the actual situation
he'll meet within his family?
Or will there be a contradiction
of his most dread and sure prediction,
more proof of that phenomenon
which I affirmed in stanza one?
In other words, what's my intention?
Will I eventually undermine?
or have my story stay in line
with my auctorial contention?
You ought to have some time to guess,
so I shall once again digress.

XXX.

Just briefly, with some information
about the Burgin family scene,
where Richard hurried from the station
(with Henriette) on May nineteen.
You've met the missus and the mister,
his oldest brother and his sister,
and now I shall the others name:
in nineteen-hundred Myron came,
not too far behind him, Paula,
and then Mateus-Teodor
and Juliusz (whom Ronia bore
within a year of one another);
and that completes the Burgin eight
who now await our graduate.

CHAPTER FIVE

The Burgins, November 1911: Left to right: Moisey, Myron (seated in front), Julek and Mateus, Lilia, Ronia, Paula, Bernard, Richard.

XXXI.

With young Bernard, and moreso, Lily,
my Richard shared the closest ties;
they were the only siblings, really,
he'd lived with, so that's no surprise.
Though when away he wondered whether
it would seem strange to be together,
"the family was so closely-knit,"[1]
he rarely was apart from it;
he was quite close to all his siblings,
from whom by travels he'd been cleft;
once home, he felt he'd never left,
and joined into their joys and quibblings
spontaneously and magically,
a limb regrown upon the tree.

XXXII.

Of course, the Burgins had their troubles;
Moisey and Ronia, you recall,
were psychologically doubles -
at once enthralled and disenthralled
with one another; yet they rarely
indulged in arguments unfairly
before the children: he would cease,
or she would tensely hold her peace.
In nineteen twelve, I ought to mention,
Moisey's finances had improved,
which put him in a better mood;
now optimistic, free from tension,
he had regained his former pluck,
his faith in self, and in his luck.

---

[1] Comment of Maria Wierna Burgin, widow of Juliusz Burgin, made to the author in August, 1981.

XXXIII.

Thus, the home on Nowolípka,[1]
when Richard crossed its threshold, rent
with guilt, *krasnéya, no s ulýbkoy*,[2]
though not ideal, was quite content.
Arrival. Amid the shouts, embracing,
excitement, and his pulse aracing,
he raised his hand for silence: 'Well,'
he paused, 'I've got great news to tell!
Please meet...' Although the unexpected
amazed and shocked them all at first,
there was no scandalous outburst;
Moisey and Ronia both respected
the rules of hospitality,
he noisily, she silently.

XXXIV. XXXV.

....
....
....
....

---

[1] Nowolípka, a main street in the Jewish section of Warsaw.
[2] *krasnéya, no s ulýbkoy* = blushing, but with a smile (Russian)

XXXVI.

Two weeks had passed. The visit, nearing
its end, had settled into calm,
my couple outwardly appearing
well-rested and without a qualm;
but, appearances can be deceiving,
and Richard found himself receiving,
through all the noisy fun and sport,
a message of the silent sort;
for all the stories, banter, blather,
chitchat, no one said a word
pro èto,[1] till, one night, he heard
his mother whispering to his father,
'You know, Moisey, this is no whim.
You'd better have a talk with him.'

XXXVII.

So on the eve of his departure,
Moisey and Richard took a walk
to. . .(oh, but reader, aren't you smart, you're
quite right about the rhyme here) talk.
Around the neighborhood they ambled,
as Moses nervously preambled
the topic, feeling out of joint,
but finally he approached the point:
'So Richard, now you plan to marry?'
'I do. I love her very much.'
'I know, my boy, but it is such
a. . .serious step, a lot to carry,
I mean, responsibility. . .'
'I realize that.' 'You won't be free,

---

[1] *pro èto*, literally, about that. A common euphemism for "about love" (Russian).

XXXVIII.
'so free, you know, I mean, it's harder. . .
a wife, and. . .children. . .to support.
That's quite a job, to keep the larder
well-stocked,' he started to exhort,
'to make a living isn't easy!'
'I know that, but, don't be uneasy;
on *that* score I feel quite secure
my job in Finland will assure
a pretty stable in-' 'Yes, Richard,
of course. And I'm so proud of you,
about the job, your mother too,
but son, we. . .[words of warning, which had
eluded him, now reached his tongue]
we feel that you. . .are just too young.'

XXXIX.
'I'm not, I'm not,' the youth insisted,
too angrily to save his pride.
'We think you are,' Moisey insisted,
'and maybe we're unjustified,
who knows? But wouldn't it be frightful
to end your visit, so delightful,
somehow estranged?' He turned his eyes
to Richard, 'So, let's compromise.'
'How?' 'Listen, I am not opposing
your getting married, nor your choice;
in fact, it makes my heart rejoice,
your happiness; I'm just proposing,
you. . .put it off a year or two,
and then, my boy, good luck to you.'

XL.

Thus once again my story hangs on
the guessing game of either-or,
but since I'm bored with tempos *langsam*,[1]
I won't suspend you as before.
He did agree to a postponement -
I don't know why—perhaps atonement?
perhaps what Ronia left unsaid?
or guilt? or what his father said?
But he gave in, and at this juncture
you may be thinking Richard's way
will follow that of Prince Andrey.*
Such sharpness normally would puncture
my muse, but her balloon is not
inflated yet with such a thought.

XLI.

Unlike Natasha, Henrietta -
and everything depends on HER -
herself believed it might be better
if their marriage were deferred.
It wasn't that she didn't love him,
or that she held herself above him,
or that she didn't want to wed,
or that she hadn't lost her head,
or was by nature too complacent.
She didn't know quite what was wrong,
except that all the very strong
emotions, and desires, nascent
within her, sometimes strangely made
her feel a little bit afraid.

---

[1] *langsam* = slow (German).

XLII.

And this confused and frightened feeling
welled up in her, and overtook
her love, when he, with eyes appealing,
would steal at her a certain look.
It seemed to her that look was gunning
her down, and she would feel like running,
so much at times it was a strain
to make the effort to remain.
His looks, she knew, were not a sin, and
she would not kill their happiness
for what she deemed her silliness,
but when she saw him off to Finland,
she sensed, beneath her parting grief,
an undercurrent of relief.

XLIII.

He journeyed forth, quite unaware of
the doubts that plagued his darling's soul;
he had his own portentous share of
anxieties about his goal.
The future alternately brightened
and then grew dim and left him frightened.
Had it been right for him to choose
to put things off, or would he lose?
A year or two—that seemed forever!
Oh, clearly he had been a fool
to let his father overrule
his own desires, and whenever
impatient thoughts like these would nag,
it seemed that time would really drag.

XLIV.

But he became so very busy,
the weeks and months flew by so fast,
that time outstripped his personal tizzy
about the year he wouldn't last,
which somehow passed before he knew it,
or even how he'd gotten through it.
His old time-tested rule, don't shirk,
and his devotion to his work
not only made the time go faster,
they brought a second, timely boon,
and really, not a mite too soon.
He was promoted concertmaster,[1]
which he was sure would save the day,
and put an end to all delay.

XLV.

And so, the Helsingfors connection,
which Richard feared would be the death
of his and Henriette's affection,
turned out to give it second breath,
at least when viewed from his perspective,
since it attained his dual objective:
material security,
and marital felicity.
He was all smiles when he told her,
and gazed, enraptured, in her eyes
to catch the love in their surprise,
and with his own to try and hold her;
but her response to his great news
had left him feeling quite confused.

---

[1] In 1914 the two Helsingfors orchestras merged into one, the Helsingfors City Orchestra, of which Burgin was concertmaster until 1916.

XLVI.

It's true that she had been excited,
very proud, and most impressed,
but asking her to marry blighted
her mood, and she became distressed.
Her manner changed to slightly ruffled,
her voice had sounded almost muffled,
and she appeared to hesitate,
when he had tried to set the date.
Her attitude had been perplexing;
although she had at last said yes,
the when was anybody's guess,
and that, you must admit, was vexing;
she seemed at once to dare and daunt;
'Good Lord,' he mused, 'what *does* she want?!'

XLVII.

Although he wouldn't have believed it,
she was as dumbfounded as he.
'To shy from bliss when you've achieved it!
How stupid can a person be!'
And though with him I'm empathetic,
to her I'm also sympathetic:
when you yourself have made things worse,
it isn't any less a curse.
It's bad enough when others muddle
things up for you, or cause the strife
which discombobulates your life,
but it is worse when *you* befuddle
yourself; the onus is the same,
but you have just yourself to blame.

XLVIII.

And endless, futile lacerating
yourself with blaming never solves,
but ends up just exacerbating
the guilt from which self-blame evolves.
Thus, my heroine capricious
whipped herself in circles vicious;
for days she whirled, a spinning top,
until she tumbled to a stop,
so dizzied by her self-derision,
and nauseated by her pain,
she could not pull the string again
to spin some more in indecision;
she'd had enough of "let it ride,"
her tailspin ended in 'Decide!'

XLIX.

Thank God. I, too, am sick of spinning
this dizzy lovers' tale of mine.
I never thought at Five's beginning
I'd get to stanza forty nine;
but that's the way it is with wimmin -
they rarely sink, but leave you swimmin'!
(although, it's also true with men
we all tread water, now and then).
But now my battle of the sexes -
to use a third stale metaphor
(a practice which I do abhor) -
with all its auguries and hexes,
its plans and obstacles and frights,
its feints and joinings and its flights

CHAPTER FIVE

L.
has ended with both parties sueing
for peace and future harmony,
and all their wearying, worried wooing
concludes in conjugality.
Alas, no memory has carried
to me the date when they were married,
but I suggest it might have been
in early spring, nineteen fourteen.
My guesswork rests upon a letter,
of four, 'fourteen, from Glazunoff;
I'll quote his words in signing off
(for my tale's end there's no proof better):
"I wish you and your wife success,
good fortune, health, and happiness."[1]

---

[1] From the end of a letter from Glazunov to Burgin, dated April 9, 1914. Original in Russian.

CHAPTER SIX: THE SCANDINAVIAN SEPARATION

The only happiness is work.
- Briusov

I.

Having sent her joyful lovers
abroad to Finnish happiness,
my muse withdrew beneath the covers
to sleep and dream of their success.
Her absence soon had left me yawning,
and fits of anxious boredom spawning;
from endless, dancing chapter five,
I felt no more than half-alive,
but it was done. So, sorely needing
a rest, I too turned down my bed;
without a rhyme inside my head,
without a bit of bedtime reading,
and with no "vision pure and deep,"
exhausted, I lay down to sleep.

II.

All was quiet. In the living-
room, curled in satisfaction fat,
her furry, faceless body heaving
noiseless breathing, slept the cat;
within the gated galley-kitchen,
horizontal, hardly twitching,
a knobby, moribund, gray log,
in deathlike stillness slept the dog;
and though the ceiling from my neighbors'
treading feet and stereo boom
no longer shook my silent room,
and night had quieted all labors,
to me sleep just refused to come;
I lay and stared in darkness dumb.

III.

By his great joy, but half-expected,
and by the smiles in her eyes,
which hid strange fears he'd not detected,
and which were merely my surmise,
I was obsessed; I simply couldn't
plot out the rest; my worry wouldn't
allow my sleepy head to nod,
as if a sharp electric prod
had shocked my brain, as if a measure-
less chasm would blacken out my head...
'My *Life* shall die,' Diana said,
'yet grief from it is somehow pleasure.
"I'm not complaining: why complain?"
One can't create without some pain.'

IV.

So onward, onward with my story!
A new direction now it takes,
through Scandinavian territory,
pursuing Burgin as he makes
a movement west. My yarn unravels
the horizontal of his travels
along the sixtieth latitude,
to ten degrees of longitude;
from Helsingfors he goes to Sweden,
but Stockholm residence is not
to be my concertmaster's lot;
his post there acted as a lead-in,
conducting him to finally play
in Christiania, Norway.

V.

Fortune charmed his westward movement;
a calm Hesperian destiny
insured professional improvement,
and Burgin, born in 'ninety three,
escaped the storms of destitution,
pogróms, world war, and revolution,
which thundered from the bellowing Beast
upon the European East.
My fate, alas, is less assuring;
to have to write a life so blessed
can make biographers distressed;
but at the risk of being boring,
I still must tell, as best I can,
the story of "a lucky man."[1]

VI.

His luck was resonant of esses;
Schnéevoigt, Strauss, Sibelius,
successively, insured successes,
sagacity, and stimulus.
His Scandinavian story centers
on reminiscence of these mentors,
but leaves unheard the silent strife
and piano of his private life.
My Scandinavian composition
attaches to his key, *Es-dur*,[2]
the unrelated *H* of pure,
though enharmonic, supposition.
My song shall hum the aitch's hush
beneath his *Es-dur* saga's shush.

---

[1] "A lucky man," Burgin's frequent assessment of his life's persona.
[2] In German, *Es-dur* is E-flat major and *H* is B major. The key of *H* is only distantly related to *Es-dur* through the enharmonic equivalency of B and C-flat.

VII.

You'll hear in *Es* semi-official
memories and anecdotes;
in *H*, some echoes interstitial
re-searched from biographic notes.
This sonorous programmatic mixture
cannot, of course, create a picture
of everything that happened then,
since much is way beyond my ken;
it only can suggest impressions -
researched, remembered, fixed, and free -
which stayed with him, occurred to me,
my hunches and his self-expressions
of six years when he'd separate,
assimilate, and emigrate.

VIII.

"In Stockholm, Helsingfors, and Oslo,
I held the concertmasterships,
and formed a string quartet, and also,
made yearly concertizing trips."
His soloistic reputation
was built on his interpretation
of Sibelius, whose advice
he sought, to make it more precise.
His wife, HB, was also active,
performing under Burgin's name
to widespread critical acclaim,
which deemed her gifted and attractive.
The Burgins seemed to be that rare
example of an ideal pair.

IX.

Our public and our private image,
however, oftentimes diverge,
and only at the line of scrimmage
at home, can they be said to merge.
The work arena's hustle-bustle
outsounds our muffled, private tussle,
and thus to others it may seem,
we both are playing on one team,
when actually we are opponents,
who struggle, maybe overmuch,
to give ourselves the lie we touch,
pretending that we are exponents
of teamed-up unity ideal,
while teeming with destruction real.

X.

This game, of course, requires players
of idiosyncratic stamp;
it's not for hotheads or dismayers,
the braggert lover or the vamp;
it's not for people who can handle,
or have a flair for public scandal,
or openly to friends express
their inner anger and distress.
This game appears designed for persons,
who cannot let their feelings out,
who feel ashamed to rave or shout,
who blush at even mild cursings,
who have to cover up the taint
of grievous rage with self-restraint.

XI.

Such a one, in conversations,
will rarely air his personal beefs,
and shuns as banal, recitations
of private troubles, woes, and griefs.
He usually refrains from stoking
his angry fire by chain-smoking,
and manifests the stubborn quirk
of calming down with anxious work;
this person often is divided
between the selves he shows the world
and keeps inside, so tightly furled,
that others think him too one-sided;
this is a person who pretends
to everyone, even best friends.

XII.

And such a man was Richard Burgin,
and such a woman—Henriette;
to friends their marriage was an érg in
the desert of their tête-à-tête,
and if their private life eluded
their intimates, I'd be deluded
to think that after all this time,
I could uncover it through rhyme.
According to the testimony
of Törnquist, Burgin's closest friend
in Stockholm, "only toward the end"
of this mysterious matrimony
"did Richard seem to be upset,
perhaps because of Henriette.

XIII.

"I thought that maybe he was seeking
divorce, perhaps it came about
in Stockholm." Here he finished speaking,
and left the matter in much doubt.
Supporting Törnquist's information
about the time of separation
are several disparate facts which came
through research: under Burgin's name
our Henrietta, post December,
nineteen sixteen, no longer played;
then, some relatives conveyed
the feeling that they could remember,
the marriage lasted just two years,
but nothing more had reached their ears.

XIV.

Finally, though this may be stretching
imagination on my part,
and blur the demarcation sketching
the boundary of life and art,
I still must quote to you, in view of
my skimpy proof, from a review of
his March first concert, 'seventeen;
you too may read beneath, between
these lines: "...a rather agitated
interpretation was given us
by Burgin of Sibelius...."[1]
I wonder, has the critic stated,
unknowingly, by chance some kind
of clue to Burgin's state of mind?

---

[1] *Stockholms-Tidningen*, Friday, March 2, 1917.

XV.

Who knows? I've clearly no solution;
I think the break-up with his wife
occurred around the Revolution,
and as for what had caused the strife,
I find the mystery fascinating,
but feel that further speculating
is out of tune with everything
that Burgin thought was interesting;
and so, enough of my reflections,
of trying my divining-rod
on Burgin's Swedish period.
He too had "vivid recollections,"
not of the break-up in his house,
but of his meeting Richard Strauss.

XVI.

"Strauss came to guest conduct in Stockholm,[1]
and had a first-rate orchestra;
that was the only place that offered
good food in those days, not *ersatz*.
That's why we had the best and sundry
musicians there, from every country,
and Strauss was happy too, you see,
to come there, and eat decently!
Ja! I've a vivid recollection -
oh, his conducting was superb!
but he was really quite reserved,
and won respect, but not affection.
I had there, though it made me wince,
an interesting experience.

---

[1] At the end of February, 1917. (DLB.)

XVII.

"I then was in my early twenties,
and pretty cocky too, you know,
and I spoke very well in German -
that was a great advantage—so,
I played *Ein Heldenleben*, and he,
though silent, let me understand he
was happy, since he could be quite
outspoken, if some thing weren't right
when others played. Well, I was cocky,
and very much less nervous than
I am now, or have been since then;
so, somehow, I got up the courage,
to ask him—hoping I'd exposed
some unclear thing which he composed -

XVIII.

"about that phrase in *Heldenleben*,
that's double for the violins,
and for, if I am not mistaken,
bass clarinet. The phrase begins:
A-sharp, inverted F-sharp major
chord, resolving to D-major -
exactly as you would expect,
all very simple and correct;
but the inversion has the bass-note,
F-sharp, which goes below our G,
and that was very strange to me!
So I'd the nerve to ask the maestro -
it was in German that we spoke -
'How, maestro, should we play this note?'

XIX.

"as if to ask for his suggestion.
His answer put me in my place:
'You know,' he said, 'this stupid question
is put so often to my face,
that I am sick and tired of it,
but seeing that you're not above it,
and such a young man, very young,
I'll ask you, what should I have done?
Should I have written, incorrectly,
G-natural, since you can't play
F-sharp? Then, you'd be right to say,
"That's wrong." Besides, you can't expect me
to let *your* lowest string confine,
and ruin this lovely, curvy line.'

XX.

"You know, for me, brought up to honor
each note, for so aspiring
a young musician, well, his answer,
quite frankly, was discouraging.
I was confused. I said, 'I'm sorry,'
but seeing that there was no more he
would say, I left. But still, you know,
his answer had disturbed me so,
for years I looked for a solution.
The F-sharp's played by clarinet,
the violins don't play it, yet
they try creating the illusion,
that there's an F-sharp there, and so,
they move their hands somewhere below

XXI.

"the G-string, make believe they're playing;
and that effect, you see, a kind
of unintentional gliss, I'm saying,
is what, I think, he had in mind.
I do not blame him for refraining
from telling me, since such explaining
should not be necessary, yet,
that, I never will forget!
You know, I've always found composers
enigmas. How do they create?
and how do they communicate,
outside of music, with musicians
they need to have their work performed,
so their intentions aren't deformed?

XXII.

"In this respect, three great composers
impressed me more than anyone;
Stravinsky, Hindemith, and Schoenberg -
I had contact with each one,
but that was when I was in Boston,
and it's a little bit exhausting
to tell these stories all at once;
besides, I think it's time for lunch."
A good idea. I'll end this portion
of Burgin's memories on tape;
my poem must retain its shape,
and I'd be guilty of distortion,
to let him sing his Boston air
before I'd even got him there.

XXIII.

And that is yet another story,
which contrapuntally we'll tell,
resounding to his greater glory,
upon the echoes of the knell,
that tolled divorce and desolation,
denial and disconsolation,
the dolorous feelings which he heard,
though never spoke of them a word.
The year when Burgin was divorcing
does not in concert dates abound,
but he was able to rebound,
in nineteen eighteen, by recoursing
to teaching, playing symphony,
and chamber group activity.

XXIV.

The latter was a gainful reason
to fight his loss of Henriette;
the nineteen-eighteen/nineteen season
enhanced the Burgin String Quartet,
which toured and played all over Sweden
and Scandinavia as the leading
contemporary chamber group.
The motley members of the troupe -
Swedish Törnquist, Burgin's fellow
fiddler; Russian-speaking Mann,
a little-known violist, and
the Finnish Kinkulin on 'cello -
all harmonized together, hiked
the group's success, and "were well-liked."[1]

---

[1] "The Quartet was successful and well-liked." (Törnquist)

The Burgin String Quartet, Stockholm, ca. 1918.

XXV.

The steady rise of Burgin's fortunes
in Sweden helped to ease the strain
of other, family misfortunes,
that must have also caused him pain;
and these, like many other troubles,
(as often noted) came in doubles:
first, the unexpected tragedy
of Paula's death, from bone TB;
and next, the news about his mother -
her health had suddenly declined,
and now to bed she was confined.
For Richard there could be no other
anxiety so torturesome;
how he wanted to be home!

XXVI.

But for the moment, there was naught he
could do, but hope that she would mend,
and work his hardest with the thought he
was earning money he could send
to Warsaw; hence, his spring decision
to try to find a new position,
so he could send more home each week.
He did not have too long to seek,
for once again, the old "ess-factor"
combined with talent, will, and pluck
to bring another bit of luck:
his chef-d'orchestre/benefactor,
Herr Schnéevoigt, sighted virgin land
to start a new orchestral band.

XXVII.

A man of energy unbounded,
for whom there was no last hurrah,
in nineteen nineteen Schnéevoigt founded
the Oslo Symphony Orchestra,
and as before in Finland, Sweden,
so in Norway, Schnéevoigt, needing
a concertmaster, forthwith thought
of Richard Burgin for the spot.
"I came to Oslo in the autumn,
and learned Norwegian so well,
that most Norwegians couldn't tell
I wasn't born there. Hanson, Thorson,
and Ibsen—every word they wrote
I read, and almost knew by rote.

XXVIII.

"When I left Russia for some country,
it always was my attitude,
to assume my stay in that new country
would not be just an interlude;
and so I tried assimilating
to that new culture, speculating
that for some length of time, you see,
I'd settle down there, hopefully."
In Oslo, though, his expectation
of permanence was not fulfilled;
some chance apparently had willed
a second, sudden, separation,
which was by spring of 'twenty near;
he stayed in Norway just one year.

XXIX.

"I had been working there with Schnéevoigt,
in Oslo, Stockholm, Helsingfors,
and we were all the time together,
and knew each other well, of course.
Well, in the summers he would often
conduct in Scheviningen, Holland.
Among the guest conductors there
in nineteen twenty was Monteux,
and he, as it turned out, was booking
for Boston; Fradkin[1] had resigned -
there'd been a fracas of some kind -
but, anyway, Monteux was looking,
and spoke to Schnéevoigt there, you see,
and Schnéevoigt recommended me.

XXX.

"He wrote—I was in London—saying,
'Although I hate to let you go,
I told Monteux about your playing;
if I'd not done that much, you know,
my conscience never would forget it.
Of course, this doesn't mean you'll get it,
but the opportunity's so rare,
I thought I ought to do my share.'
Well that was really very nice, and
he said till such-and-such a date
Monteux's in Paris, don't delay.'
And so I took Schnéevoigt's advice, and
I went to Paris right away -
some friends invited me to stay

---

[1] Fradkin, the concertmaster of the Boston Symphony Orchestra, who resigned at the end of the 1919–20 season. Monteux's appointment as conductor of the orchestra was to begin in the fall, 1920.

XXXI.

"who had arrived from Russia lately.
I played for Monteux in his home;
he told me that unfortunately,
on piano, he can just play some,
well, harmonies, once in a while,
since he plays badly. Then he smiled,
and asked, 'What would you like to play?
Tchaikovsky? Beethoven? Please say!'
You know, the standard repertory.
I played this, that, then this, you see,
for forty minutes, approximately.
He didn't bother me, or worry
about orchestral music, since
he knew I had experience

XXXII.

"with Schnéevoigt several years already.
I'd better tell him, though, I thought,
till then I had performed a steady
Germanic repertoire. 'I'm not,'
I said, 'outside of Strauss, not very
familiar with contemporary
composers,' and that there were few
French works, or modern things, I knew.
He said, 'That isn't too alarming.
I too don't know them, but I hope
together we'll enlarge our scope.'
Well, that was very nice and charming!
He clearly liked the way I played,
and said to go back, right away,

XXXIII.

"to London, where a Mr. Bremen,
the manager, was, and to sign
a contract—once I got a permit,
which was not easy at that time.
Somehow, however, I succeeded,
went to London, signed the needed
papers, and, that was the way
I was engaged by him to play."

....
....
....
....
....
....

XXXIV.

Now that we have reached the moment
when Burgin's future die was cast,
perhaps the time has come to comment,
in general, on the life that's past.
His marriage and his youth now over,
my Burgin, concertmastering rover,
aboard the Bergensfjord, awaits
a new life in the United States.
So as he sails across the ocean,
let's scan the past he's left behind,
(which he might too have called to mind):
the joys and sorrows, calms, commotion,
the ordinary and bizarre
events that marked his life thus far.

XXXV.

Before I turn reflection inward,
and dabble in psychology
(a ticklish business!), I'll begin with
a try at physiognomy.
His red-cheeked face, complected fairish,
was oval-chinned, high-browed, and squarish,
half circled in brown, wavy hair;
his nose curved down below the flare
of nostrils with its base inverting
in shape his delicate upper lip,
its pointed peaks and center dip;
the lower one, more self-asserting,
and thicker, often would jut out,
when he would concentrate or pout.

XXXVI.

But Burgin's most attractive feature
was deepset eyes of hazel-gray;
their glances were a silent teacher
of what he said, and didn't say:
they beamed awide to share your pleasure,
in narrowed calm they took your measure,
their distant stare would often seem
to tell about some private dream;
a downcast glance conveyed, 'That's vile,'
a gentle glow expressed, 'You're dear,'
a glaze—'I'm bored,' a dimming—fear,
but best of all those eyes could smile;
no other eyes could shine so bright
with joy, surprise, or pure delight.

XXXVII.

So, when, at almost twenty-seven,
he pondered all he'd undergone,
what happenings would memory leaven?
who might he smile back upon?
Wiśniewski, Lotto, and Joachim;
the day that Auer thundered át him;
Jascha's *pizzicato* scales,[1]
Boris's quips and Mischa's tales;
Pávlovsk, where he had "discovered" -
when he had thought he was so smart -
the *Kreutzer* had a piano part!
and all the pieces he'd uncovered,
which no one else had heard as yet;
the great success of his quartet,

XXXVIII.

his marvellous luck in Scandinavia,
the charming people he had met -
'Schnéevoigt, my colleague, friend, and savior!
How many jobs he helped me get!
And Törnquist, Stenhammar,* Grevillius,*
Hannikainnen,* Sitt,* Sibelius,
and Strauss—I never will forget. . .
[his smile tinged now with regret]
that strange F-sharp in *Heldenleben*,
a real enigma!. . . but, why fret?
I'll find an explanation yet -
it's not like. . .oh, *hör auf zu beben*![2]
[he stared, then lit a cigarette]. . .
it isn't like. . .my Henriette.'

---

[1] Reference to a lesson of the young Heifetz which Burgin was present at, when the *Wunderkind* astounded Auer with his flying pizzicato.

[2] "Hör auf zu beben" (Cease trembling), from the final movement of Mahler's Second Symphony ("Resurrection"). Burgin became acquainted with Mahler's music while he was still a student, his introduction to the composer being the Fourth Symphony: "That was very new, and that is an impression I have never forgotten. Since that time, I was just crazy about Mahler. Nobody existed but Mahler." (Richard Burgin)

XXXIX.

He smiled as the tears were welling,
and felt a lump inside his throat,
as if some inner voice were quelling
the urge to sing so sad a note.
It was a very strange sensation,
half-solace and half-desolation,
to keep on smiling as you sigh,
and feel like laughing when you cry.
He felt so tragic, yet the comic
would sometimes syncopate his grief;
from sadness smiles brought relief.
To this mixed motion metronomic
came memories of *those* two years,
with rueful smiles through the tears.

XL.

If you can contemplate the wreck of
your happiness with smiling gaze,
you're playing quite in tune with Chekhov,
and might be acting out his plays,
in which, 'tis said, hearts break from battle
behind the teacups' muted rattle,
and where the lovelorn have the quirk
of burying sadness in their work.
The selfsame smiles mark his stories
wherever wrongs have no redress,
and people cope with their distress
by pasting smiles on their worries:
they rise, work hard, and go to bed,
survive their lives, and look ahead.

XLI.

They hope the future will be better,
like Doctor Astrov,[1] they avow,
the human race will break its fetters,
about two hundred years from now.
Their present woes have no solution,
but they have hope, in evolution;
in nature there is permanence,
a pledge of one's continuance.
The only comfort comes from working:
you plant your garden, help it grow,
and though its progress may be slow,
there's no excuse in that for shirking,
for if you quit, give into gloom,
your plants will surely never bloom.

XLII.

Some say that Chekhov is depressing:
they find his viewpoint a dead-end,
dislike him for his not expressing
the faith that mortals will transcend,
that there's a heaven for achievers,
eternal life for true believers,
a comforting embrace above
for those betrayed by earthly love.
Some readers think it meretricious,
and for a Russian writer odd,
to put more hope in work than God,
while others just find work suspicious,
or cannot cope, or lack all hope,
and thus do nothing, except dope.

---

[1] In Chekhov's play *Uncle Vanya*.

XLIII.

But Chekhov also has defenders,
(I count myself among their group),
who run to work from their offenders,
and somehow manage to recoup;
who try to focus on the antic
in youthful debacles romantic,
and realize, once they've had their cry,
that life goes on (though who knows why?);
who do not doubt that on the trek of
existence, everyone has woes,
youth flowers, and away it goes,
and through their tears they read their Chekhov,
and smile, 'How wonderfully he
depicts my own reality!'

XLIV.

It may appear that this digression
has taken me quite far afield,
but I have tried to give expression
to certain thoughts I hoped would yield
some inner truths about my hero;
of course, it's possible that zero
in Chekhov's writing would obtain
to Burgin, and I've waxed in vain,
yet I have got this stubborn notion -
a sign of madness, to be sure -
that somehow Russian literature
will serve me up a magic potion,
which, if I drink sufficiently,
will make my hero known to me.

XLV.

And that is why Tolstoy provided
the aims and atmosphere of *Youth*;
by Dostoevsky I was guided
in hearing Burgin's silent truth;
First Love combined Tolstoy's Irteniev,[1]
with Pushkin's Tanya, and Turgenev;
and poets of the Silver Age
conveyed the ambience of each stage;
and now, on Burgin's separation
from youth and Europe, on the brink
of his maturity, I think
his real and bookish maturation
have formed a new American
of character Chekhovian.

XLVI.

But that's to come. Though I sincerely
am moved to tell my hero's fate,
my muse has fixed her mute, and clearly
for now his *Life* will have to wait.
Towards academic prose inclining,
a deadline's dampering my rhyming,
and I—with some regret, it's true -
"more lazily my verse pursue."[2]
I do not feel the old desires
for scribbling Onegin reams;
other frigid, numbing dreams,
other choking, smoking fires,
in light of day and night's black hole,
disturb the harmony of my soul.

---

[1] Irteniev, the hero of Tolstoy's *Youth*.
[2] Quoted from Pushkin, *Eugene Onegin*, Six, XLIII.

XLVII.

I've felt the gasp of jerky measures,
I've heard a new unstable key,
arhythmia pants of fewer pleasures,
and rues the old tonality.
O Harmony, where is your rigor?
and where, its perfect-rhyming, *vigor*?
Is it really true at last
its joyful season now is past?
Can it be factually attested,
without august encomion
the springtime of my life is gone
(as often up till now I've jested)?
And can it be there's no return?
and I shall shortly forty turn?

XLVIII.

Well, then, complaints are unbecoming
my Apollonian design,
for life's a balance—going, coming -
so fare thee well, o youth of mine!
I thank you for your sweet euphorias,
your nightmarish phantasmagorias,
your larks and lulls, your lows and lifts;
for all your losses and your gifts
you have my gratitude. With you I
had many a worry and a thrill,
of Dionysus drank my fill;
enough! now curious for the new I
set out again, to try my best,
and from your storm and fury rest.

XLIX.

Just one look back. Goodbye, scenarios,
in which I've acted to the hilt
second-stringers, impresarios,
my dreams, anxieties, and guilt.
But you, capricious inspiration,
excite my poor imagination,
buy me a seventh Ball-Liner pen,
and come to visit in my den.
Don't leave the poet in destitution,
to sit and scribble all alone,
or worse, embittered, turn to stone
in some dream-deadening institution
of learning, where, like all my friends,
I must earn means to gain your ends.

CHAPTER SEVEN: IN THE NEW WORLD

My city and country as I am Antonius,
is Rome; as a man, the whole world.

- Marcus Aurelius

Die liebe Erde allüberall
Blüht auf im Lenz und grunt aus neu!
Allüberall und ewig blauenlicht die
Fernen!
Ewig, ewig...ewig, ewig...

- Gustav Mahler

How saddened am I by your coming,
o spring, spring! Time of love!

- A. S. Pushkin

I.

Chased by sultry southwest breezes,
April suddenly retreats;
the first May warming Cambridge seizes
to dress in green its naked streets.
Overnight, without a warning,
the bud-eyes pop to greet year's morning;
washed, but still half-dressed, the trees
urge on their sleepy limbs, 'Oh, please!
You're late, so hurry with your greening!
Forsythia's already out,
clipped lawns and waxy hedges shout,
in geometric patterns preening,
"The Spring is here."[1] Its painful birth
revives from dreams the song of earth.

---

[1] "The Spring is here," from "The Drunkard in Spring," *The Song of the Earth* (Mahler).

II.

How saddened am I by your coming,
oh spring! the season of farewell!
What morbid memories stirs the humming
of *ewig*[1] which your songs foretell!
With what mute fear I mishear 'never,'
in that repeated faint 'forever'
of your "horizon glimmering blue,"
and of your earth "grown green anew."
What is it? Can it be your pleasures,
and everything that freshens, gives
to earthly life delight, relives
the pulse of Mahler's dying measures
I heard conducted long ago
by one whose death bereaved me so?

III.

Or is it, rueing the renewal
of verdure soon to fade next fall,
I find ironic spring too cruel,
and wonder why it blooms at all?
Or is my anguish just endemic
to my profession academic,
the springtime urge for lazy fun
reminding me my work's undone?
Perhaps too often I remember,
in moments lackadaisical,
the start of my sabbatical,
my *Life's* beginning in November,
and now that it is nearly grown,
recall the spring when it was sown.

---

[1] *ewig* = forever (German).

IV.

That was the April he lay dying,
but when his daughter came to life -
belatedly, there's no denying -
and jogged the memory of his wife,
preserved the stories she had lost, and
returned to try to résearch Boston.
Spring called me to the archives then!
A time of studious regimen,
a time of gathering information,
of taking notes, transcribing tapes,
and dreaming out the narrative shapes
for facts, surmises, inspiration.
That springtime blossomed with a task
allowing grief to wear a mask.

V.

The future makes my muse downhearted.
Indulge her fondness for the past,
my patient reader! Let's get started!
I'm ready to begin at last.
Let's go to where my muse feels freer
to rhyme a musical career,
to Massachusetts Avenue,
to Symphony Hall, where Burgin, new
in Boston when he came in 'twenty,
became a fixture on the stage,
conducting, playing, till the age
of sixty nine; where he left plenty
of gifts behind for those he got,
but where today, of course, he's not.

Richard Burgin at the time of his arrival in the United States.

VI.

It's April, 'eighty one; we're taking
a special, very private tour
of Symphony Hall, and therefore, making
our entrance by the side stage-door.
Descending deeply to the basements,
we walk beneath the window casements,
circuitously fathoming
the cellars of the newest wing.
There in a room, alone, surrounded
by dusty tomes, my Slavist sits,
scans old reviews for novel bits,
her vigor seemingly unbounded,
and tape-records the ones she needs;
let's take a look at what she reads:

VII.

SYMPHONY'S NEW CONCERTMASTER,
Violinist of Renown,
Richard Burgin, Born In Warsaw,
Joins Orchestra. By Olin Downes.[1]
(I swear, to rhyme gazette descriptions
is worse than Latinate prescriptions,
which Byron managed to enshrine -
but then, he had a longer line!)
The critic gives his first impression:
"Precocity he has survived
quite well indeed; he's frank, blue-eyed,
brown-haired, and has a fair complexion."
He then describes his interview,
which I shall re-enact for you.

---

[1] *The Boston Post*, October 1, 1920.

VIII.[1]

D: Does America seem different
 from the first time you were here?
B: Yes! it's really very different,
 it is—how do you say?—so dear!
D: True! the dollar dwindles faster
 each day...Well, you're a concertmaster
 of broadly-based experience;
 I'm sure the Boston audience
 would like to know your views on music.
B: For me, there only are two kinds -
 good, and bad. I also find
 I like some music that's not music
 perhaps. I'm fascinated by
 the late works of Ravel, though I

IX.

 would say that's color more than music.
 I like some Strauss, but do not care
 for *Don Quixote*, *Zarathustra*,
 and the *Domestica*, for there
 his music is too programmatic.
 Don Quixote tells dramatic
 adventures, *and*, if you mistake
 which scene he wants to illustrate,
 then you're all wrong. Then you are kissing
 the wrong girl in the dark. To me,
 that's moving pictures which we see
 by hearing them. I'm not dismissing
 such music, but its place withal
 is scarcely in a concert hall.

---

[1] In this version of the interview, Downes' questions are imagined, and Burgin's answers are, more or less, direct quotations of Downes' quotation of them.

X.

D: Don't you think there's some reflection
in music, though it be impure,
of other arts? Or some connection
with painting, or with literature?

B: Of course, there is. But influences,
which art, or writing, evidences
at one time, say, are felt by us
in music much, much later. Thus,
the nineties saw a generation
of painters like Ravel, and though
we have so-called Cubísts[2] now, no
Cubíst-composer's in circulation.
No doubt he'll come soon, but to ask
if he'll be welcome, is not our task.

XI.

D: Indeed! Well, since we're speaking
of Europe, more specifically,
what country do you think is seeking
the most advancement, musically?

B: Undoubtedly I should say Russia.
No other country now has such a
large group of innovators, who
are looking forward. This is true,
as well, of Finland's Jean Sibelius,
whose nineteen fourteen symphony,
the *Fifth*, revised quite recently,
is even more impressionistic,
more striking, newer, and so forth,
than his extraordinary *Fourth*.

---

[2] The stress on *Cubíst* reflects Burgin's Russian pronunciation.

XII.

D: What of France? B: Certain Frenchmen
    are showing new, astonishing
    perceptions worthy of attention.
D: This has been most interesting.
    Have you time for one more question?
B: Please! D: What is your impression
    of Europe's orchestras today?
B: Well, since the war, I'd have to say,
    there's just not any that can cope with
    America's. In Germany,
    they are old men now, principally,
    and there is nothing any longer
    in Europe like the BSO.
D: Well, on that note, I'll let you go.

XIII.

Once such questions had been fielded,
Burgin started to perform.
The Symphony archives also yielded
reviews, which judged above the norm
his early efforts soloistic;
but nothing can be less artistic,
in musical *Lives*, than quoting such
reviews of concerts overmuch,
and it would really be too boring
to cite in full the praise and blame,
evaluating Burgin's fame,
in every critical outpouring;
so I'll be brief, and give instead
a summary of those I read.

XIV.

The Boston critics' view composite
of Burgin, up to 'twenty nine,
allows my teacher-self to posit
the final judgment, 'very fine';
this includes consideration
of Burgin's bearing, intonation,
technique, enthusiasm, zeal,
and his musicianly appeal,
as indicated by his playing
the violin concertos of
Tchaikovsky, Brahms, and Glazunoff
(the latter two to the inveighing
of some who thought them "jaded" then),
Sibelius, and Beethoven.

XV.

About his tone there's disagreement:
some call it "lustrous," others—"wan";
but there is positive agreement
on his "musicianly élan."
They deemed him "noble," "enthusiastic,"
"tempermental," but not bombastic,
"convincing," "musical," and "free
of crass sentimentality";
of bearing "youthful," "unpretentious,"
he sounds "the Golden pleasant mean,"
is technically "accomplished," "clean,"
and always "thoughtful, conscientious,"
"subordinates his efforts, to
produce ensemble-playing true."

XVI.

In sum, a violinist "tasteful,"
"unwaveringly accurate,"
"refined," "authoritative," "graceful,"
"unmanneredly delicate";
"romantic," but "not egoistic,"
"not virtuosic," but "artistic,"
"sincere," "painstaking," "very clear,"
"euphonious," "pleasing to the ear,"
"effective," "virile," "deft," "resilient,"
"straightforward," "energetic," "light,"
"incisive," "unaffected," "bright,"
"unclouded," "polished," "sterling," "brilliant,"
"remarkable," "intelligent,"
"scholarly," and "excellent."

XVII.

I'm sure there's no one who could rival,
now that my appraisal's done,
its subject, and its adjectival
assessing-prolegomenon.
Despite the scholarly abuses
(quotes out-of-context), it has uses:
my catalogue of adjectives,
although a bit one-sided, gives
to any teacher who is frantic
about the "recs" he has to write -
a task of dubious delight -
a list of positive semantic
descriptive qualities to choose,
with which no applicant can lose.

XVIII.

Before you chide me as a cynic,
just ponder the descriptive word;
it is by nature polygynic -
one finds it marrying a herd
of substantives, from which quintessence,
it swells and puffers, an excrescence
(in essence, there is little doubt)
nine-tenths its mates can do without.
A virile adjective is handy
for painting a lackluster house,
or livening up a barren spouse,
but every one of them's a dandy,
attracting twins to his renown,
and overburdening his noun.

XIX.

And the most burdensome and fickle,
are adjectives of ardent praise;
their object's vanity they tickle,
but leave its essence in a haze.
Although it's meant to be upraising,
there is an irony in praising:
it isn't funny when it's sparse,
but in excess, it seems a farce.
Still more ironic is invective:
we're tickled by laconic, sharp
assaults, but if the critics harp,
we're almost forced to be protective
of egos they obliterate,
and suffer those we think third-rate.

XX.

But to continue this digression,
ironically, might undermine
the praises which received expression
in Burgin's case, and misalign
my reader's trust. I need not mention,
that it was never my intention,
to drown in adjective-excéss
my hero's talent and success.
From his Bostonian beginning,
the critics note, "when he appeared
as soloist, his colleagues cheered,"
and the audiences, grinning,
"would repeatedly recall
him to the stage of Symphony Hall."

XXI.

Yet solos were for him a sideline;
his most important function was,
as concertmaster, helping guide fine
performance with the orchestra's
conductor, thus effecting concert
of boss and men, some more than ónce hurt
by the former's vents of spleen -
rehearsing, maestros can get mean.
The concertmaster is a leader,
content to seem as if he's led,
who plays two parts to get ahead -
the promulgator and the pleader;
withal, the dauntless diplomat,
which Burgin was a master at.

XXII.

During forty years of service,
with three conductors Burgin worked,
and though at moments he was nervous,
he rarely showed that he was irked.
First came Monteux; then Koussevitzky -
the latter, prone to temper fits, he
relied quite often on the balm
of Burgin's friendship to calm down -
and finally, Munch, less roused to anger,
who hated to rehearse, and fought
his battles mainly at *balot*,[1]
but could express a peevish languor,
when a rehearsal would begin,
if Burgin hadn't let him win.

XXIII.

But archives don't give information,
or at the most, not very much,
about professional relations,
dependent on a personal touch.
Thus, having reaped her public harvest
of adjectives and dates, my Slavist,
bemoaning that her primary horse
mouthed words no longer, sought a source
to plough his work life's inner furrows.
Books failed her, but, by happenstance,
October brought those tapes of Dann's,
and in their memories she burrows.
Those tapes, as one can clearly see,
have been a lifesaver for me.

---

[1] *balot*, a French card game.

XXIV.

"Monteux," thus Burgin recollected,
"could not play any instrument,
but his inner ear was perfect,
and heard just how the music went.
The score he studied really só well,
that even at the first rehearsal
of something new, we'd be amazed -
he'd spot the tiniest mistakes. . .
I still recall how I reacted,
in 'twenty two, when he put on
Stravinsky's *Sacre de Printemps*,
and I first played it. Well, I acted,
for weeks, as if I didn't know
what happened in the world, you know.

XXV.

"It was as if a revolution
has taken place in me, but I
was in a state of dissolution,
and could not pinpoint how or why.
I knew it was very tremendous -
life's not the same now; those stupendous
sounds, those rhythms, the polý-
tonality were new to me.
The general drive, oh, every measure
just stirred me; not that I could say
I liked or disliked it—it was way
beyond a thing like personal pleasure;
it was—some thing phenomenal
has happened in the music world.

XXVI.

"We had a lot of preparation;
Monteux knew *Sacre* inside out,[1]
and then, before our unionization,
no one gave a thought about
rehearsal time. He had the power
to rehearse each day for seven hours;
you simply did it; no one dared
to say a word, because we shared
the sense this manner of presenting
a piece of music was a first;
in fact, we felt we could rehearse
it even longer, not resenting
the extra time, that it was *so*,
a *very* important thing, you know."

XXVII.

If symphonic revolution,
in 'twenty two, was wrought by spring,
then, orchestral evolution
the fall of 'twenty four would bring.
Monteux resigned from his position,
and was replaced by a musician
of early virtuoso fame;
a bassist who achieved a name,
as impressario and conductor,
first in Russia, then in France;
a man of great exhuberance,
and very powerful *kharákter*,[2]
a charismatic demiurge,
whose name was: Koussevitzky, Serge.

---

[1] Monteux had conducted the world-premier in Paris, 1913 (DLB).
[2] *kharákter* = character, personality (Russian).

XXVIII.

"When Koussevitzky came to Boston,
he needed quite a bit of help.
His brilliant gift depended *most* on
his intuition, not a wealth
of learning in his own profession;
and in a way, it's my impression,
that's what really made him great.
His talent he'd communicate
in spite of lacks in education.
He had shortcomings, like us all,
but more important, overall,
he had conviction, imagination.
For players such a man's a czar,
no matter how cynical they are.

XXIX.

"He really tried to take good care of
the members of the orchestra,
and always tried to be aware of
what each musician's worries are;
he had a sort of father's pride in
his players, always took their side in
their gripes with management, so they
would try to go out of their way
to do whatever he'd require.
The give and take, despite his whims,
between the orchestra and him
was just the best you could desire,
and very few conductors guested,
because he called that his *orkestr*."

XXX.

And Burgin was *his* concertmaster,
at least when all was said and done;
he took the part his life had casted,
and to Koussey he played son,
a role in which he had much training,
some thirty years now of restraining
his temperment from reckless rants
to gain harmoniously his wants;
a trying role, since he was cocky,
and clearly wanted to impress
his new conductor with his success;
thus their relations had a rocky
start, and got so out of joint,
that Burgin, proud, "was on the point

XXXI.

"of handing in his resignation
during that first season, but
arrived at reconciliation"[1]
(according to the scuttle-butt).
How like the love-and-hate attractions,
and sometimes troubled interactions
with fathers of those moderate sons,
not like Bazarov, but the ones,
who being softer, like Arkady,*
at first rebel and foment strife,
but soon reject the rebel's life:
he makes his peace, and working hárd he
is quite content to settle down
and father his papá's renown.

---

[1] Quoted from Moses Smith, *Koussevitzky*.

XXXII.

So Burgin "reached an understanding
with his new chief, and from then on,"
in cases of misunderstanding,
"he was the effective liaison
between the boss and the musicians."
His talent, tact, shrewd intuitions,
and skill bore fruit, when "he became
in fact, as he'd become in name,
the BSO's Assistant conductor."[1]
(I'd add, my hero had to thank,
besides his tact, for this new rank,
that ineluctable instructor,
who had, so many years before,
conduced to *takt*[2] a child of four.)

XXXIII.

For surely, reader, you remember
how Richard's talent was found out -
that Warsaw concert where a member
of the audience had pointed out
to Moses that his son was waving
his arms in rhythm and behaving
'as if he were conducting too.'
(If not, you should *One/V* review!)
Thus, after years of observation,
redress in concertmaster's guise,
and, as his library testifies,
considerable self-education,
his old conducting gifts unfurled
in Boston's musical new world.

---

[1] Quotations in XXXII from Moses Smith.
[2] *takt* = time, beat, measure (Russian).

XXXIV.

The unfurling, though, of an Assistant
Conductor, spreads at gentle pace,
since with the maestro's co-existent,
it must not crowd that flower's space.
"My programs had to pass inspection
by Koussevitzky. My selection
of works was always fitted to
the ones he did, and planned to do."
Adapting to environmental
restrictions, hardy Burgin's bloom,
in search no doubt of *Lebens*-room,
grew out in some experimental
directions, bringing to the air
new works, such as *Pierrot Lunnaire.*

XXXV.

"By Schoenberg I was just awestricken,
both by the man, and by his work;
I studied hard what he had written, -
that was, you know, a whole new world.
Well, then, in 'twenty eight, some patrons,
elite Bostonians and matrons,
liked sponsoring *private* concerts of
new works, worthwhile works above
the ordinary. I succeeded
in getting these people to agree
to put *Lunnaire* on *publically.*
They gave me the support I needed,
and after having weeks rehearsed,
we put that on, a Boston first."

XXXVI.

As, reader, you've no doubt expected,
judging by what's gone before,
there is an anecdote connected
with this event. "In 'thirty four,
when Schoenberg came,"[1] said my recounter,
"I had with him my first encounter.
Before the Cambridge concert, he
sent up and asked to speak with me.
I thought, 'It's probably last instructions
that I should give, before we begin.'
I quickly took my violin,
went down, and based on my deductions,
I asked, 'What would you have me say?'
He says, 'It's not about today's

XXXVII.

'performance. I just heard you've done my
Pierrot Lunnaire some time ago?'
'Yes.' 'Was it difficult to put on?' 'Why,
of course, it's difficult, as you know.'
'How much rehearsal?' 'More than twenty.'
'Where was it?' 'Jordan Hall.' 'How many
does that hall seat?' 'Twelve hundred in all.'
'Oh that was much too big a hall!'
And now comes what I must consider
my, *the* most stupid repartee,
maybe of the century,
because I was by him awestricken.
I said, to make him placable,
'Maèstro, *es war nur halb-voll*!'[2]

---

[1] Schoenberg was invited to Boston by the BSO to conduct the orchestra. The first concert was in Sanders Theatre, Cambridge [DLB].
[2] *es war nur halb-voll* = it was just half-full (German).

XXXVIII.

'Thank goodness!' he replied, thus easing
my obvious embarrassment.
'But can it be you find so pleasing
a half-filled house?' 'Yes, I'm content.
You know, I doubt quite seriously whether
there're more than six hundred altogether
who'd like that piece. A full-house there,
would mean six hundred who'd hate *Lunnaire*,
and let me tell you, nothing's worse than
to sit beside a person, who
just hates what's interesting to you;
I've sat beside that type of person,
who hates my work with all his might,
it almost ended in a fight!''

XXXIX.

Your ears, dear reader, were accosted
by Burgin's anecdote to keep
my promises, but I'm exhausted,
with stanzas to go before I sleep.
My Slavist has at length reflected
on Burgin's work, but has neglected
his personal life and views; perhaps
she ought to try to fill these gaps.
Of little help her usual sources -
her library books and transcribed tapes -
and she must look some other place.
So, like Tatiana,* she recourses
to Burgin's library, where she looks
for him by leafing through his books.

XL.

The numerous scores, I need not mention,
to her but little did impart;
nor did she pay too much attention
to textbooks on conducting art.
The search seemed hopeless, and Diana
would doubt the methods of Tatiana,
and wondered, 'Why this bookish fuss?'
but then she found...Aurelius.
Whole sections of his *Meditations*
on nature, feeling, and the mind,
our Burgin, once, had underlined,
and made some marginal notations,
like rules to which he would adhere,
e.g. 'in thoughts be clean and clear.'

XLI.

Encouraged, she continued searching,
and in Descartes's philosophy,
again she saw his pencil lurching
beneath the thoughts on clarity,
and found more marginal inscriptions,
her father's earnest self-prescriptions:
when positively he'd react,
he'd make a note on how to act.
But though she felt that she was nearing
her father's mind, neither Descartes,
nor Marcus, could reveal his heart;
she knew some family tales, but fearing
she might, in telling them, abuse
his privacy, she sought my muse.

XLII.

My muse, not generally jealous
of privacy, persauded her
that she was being over-zealous;
'It won't disgrace his character,'
she mocked, 'to talk about his worries,
and even loves, or tell some stories
about his friends and family!
I think you're too damn scholarly!'
'Perhaps,' my Slavist said, retiring;
'so, what if I allow you to
relate such things—at least, a few?'
'I'm happy to.' 'But be inspiring,
or failing that, just do your best.'
'*Mais certainement*! Now go and rest.'

XLIII.

Though Burgin was a workaholic
(no doubt a family disease!),
he was not alien to frolic,
and knew what put his nerves at ease.
When pressures from his job would hárass,
he found relief from them in Paris,
where he spent several summers in
the twenties, playing violin,
but also (Juliusz[1] said) the dandy,
and most successfully, roulette.
The winnings he would often get
delighted him, and came in handy;
he played his "system," as a rule,
and never ever lost his cool.

---

[1] Juliusz Burgin, Richard's youngest brother.

XLIV.

"In 'twenty five," recalled Marysia,[1]
"your father took mamá and me
to Paris, and we met there this, ah,
a woman friend of his, you see.
A millionairess with a fancy
estate, and daughter my age, Nancy;
their park there had, to my surprise,
stuffed animals of real-life size!
Yes, she had millions, and her villa
was absolutely *élégant*. . .
They'd serve us supper on a long
and splendid table, all on silver,
and after supper, mamá would go
with Richard to a *casino*."

XLV.

Aha! I hear my love-starved readers -
ils pour l'amour toujours ont faim -
becoming hankering, hungry pleaders,
beseeching me, *cherchez la femme!*
And since I share their pangs completely
(albeit, somewhat more discretely),
I'll tell you her identity:
Louisa Fletcher Connely.*
From Indiana, she was carried
(by intellect) away to Smith,[2]
and then (by heart) to marriage with
Booth Tarkington. The match miscarried,
and four years after their divorce,
she married Connely* (of course).

---

[1] Marysia Morawski, daughter of Burgin's sister, Lily, was born in 1922 in Warsaw. She is now living in Vienna.
[2] Smith College, from which Louisa Fletcher graduated in 1900. She was ten years older than Connely, her second husband, and fifteen years older than Burgin.

XLVI.

Louisa liked creative, vital,
intelligent, and younger men.
A Boston poetess, her title,
The Land of Beginning Again,
appeared about when Burgin's history
began with her[1] —oh, what a mystery!
It's clear, however, she was rich,
until the Crash, because of which
she lost ten thousand she'd invested
in houses Burgin's uncle[2] built;
and Burgin paid her back, from guilt,
or just because he so detested
to be in anybody's debt,
especially someone he'd upset.

XLVII.

For it is clear that she was crazy
about our hero, and pursued
him, calling forth a none-too-hazy
remembrance of *his* attitude
to Henriette, and of his torment,
when that beloved's love was dormant;
because, you see, it's also clear,
though disappointing to you, I fear,
while Mrs. Connely was frantic,
and absolutely *engagée*,
my Mr. Burgin couldn't repay
the principle of her romantic
investment in him, or pretend
to interest more than for a friend.

---

[1] *The Land of Beginning Again* was published in Boston, 1921.
[2] Burgin's uncle, Leib (Leo) Burgin, built several duplexes on the Jamaicaway in Jamaica Plain, in which Burgin invested heavily and urged Mrs. Connely to invest in.

XLVIII.

Was he aware of this reversal,
so true in matters of the heart,
by which first love is one's rehearsal
for playing someone else's part?
Had his failed love with Henrietta
convinced him passion was a fetter,
so he Louisa's heart refused
to keep his own from being bruised?
Or was it that he sought from other,
especially older, women love
to compensate his wanting of
the missing woman, namely, mother?
Or did he somehow wish to hide,
the moreso after Ronia died,

XLIX.

in 'twenty six, the greatest sadness
of all his thirty three odd years,
in agape's platonic gladness,
calming thus his orphan fears?
Was it one, or all, these reasons?
or just Love's ever-changing seasons?
I only know he told his son,[1]
"the best thing I have ever done
was being almost ever-present
at my mother's bedside for
a week before she died." (O Lord,
must death in love be omnipresent?)
Enough! I've gotten back again
to that sad land where I began.

---

[1] Burgin's son, Richard Weston Burgin, was born in 1947.

L.

But I shall end with Burgin living,
in 'thirty, on Jamaicaway.
If he were home, he might be giving
a lesson, pacing, *engagé*...
but now he stops, and while explaining,
lights up beside the stand containing
his Chesterfields, a large supply,
depacked, because he likes them dry;
or maybe he is in the kitchen
with Myron,[1] just returned from class,
debating hotly over a glass
of steaming tea, his eyebrows twitching,
the national economy,
and what it means, politically.

LI.

If he weren't home, and it were morning,
or afternoon, you'd find him at
the Hall, with diligence performing
his musical trade, or failing that,
catch up with him at the dispersal,
enroute to a quartet rehearsal;
and evenings, were he concert-free,
and not with friends or family,
our very busy concertmaster
would be inside the Cavendish,[2]
fulfilling there his secret wish
to play the amateur Grand Master.
And so in life he moved along,
content on cards, strong tea, and song.

---

[1] Myron immigrated in 1925, earned his Ph.D. in Economics at Harvard, and lived with Richard in Jamaica Plain.
[2] Cavendish, the bridge club in Boston to which Burgin belonged.

LII.

I'll leave you with this new-world picture
of Burgin, newly naturalized
in 'twenty eight, an old-new mixture
of callings newly synthesized:
conductor, concertmaster, teacher,
bridge-player, veteran overreacher,
debater, didact, *raconteur*,
paternalistic bachelor,
survivor of some most distressful,
if ordinary growing pains -
some losses, but tremendous gains;
he'd been so lucky and successful,
what possible further happiness
could lie ahead? He couldn't guess. . .

Richard Burgin, 1930s.

CHAPTER EIGHT: DOUBLE CONCERTO

> *The Seventh Annual Meeting of Friends of the BSO on Nov. 5, 1940 at 4 p.m. featured Bach's Concerto For Two Violins...*
>
> *- BSO Program Book*
>
> *My ballad's theme is he and she -*
> *Not terribly new of me.*
>
> *- Mayakovsky*

I.

In those days, when I was living
on Plympton Street, I was at peace,
had gotten tenure, and was giving
my joy to teacherly release;
in those days, my preparations
for classes (versified translations
of lyric Russian poetry)
first conjured up my muse to me.
My dark apartment (not idyllic!)
was lightened by her bubbly wit,
at first, she parodied a bit,
burlesqued Tolstoy in rhymes dactyllic,
then into verse perversely chose
to put my academic prose.

II.

With idiosyncratic "Myshkin"
to Howard Keller we laid siege;
to our surprise he took the risk in
accepting it to appear in SEEJ.[1]

....
....
....
....
....
....
....
....
....
....

III.

Last autumn we began the present
half-humorous, half-serious work;
at first my muse was rather hesitant
to show the world my latest quirk,
but vanity at last induced her
to strut her stuff. I introduced her
amidst the friendly noise and glee
of Friday Night Society,[2]
and like a tippler, she cavorted,
and sang a chapter over wine;
the faces of those friends of mine
with tearful laughter were contorted.
Oh I admit that I was proud
to share her with the Friday crowd!

---

[1] SEEJ, *The Slavic and East European Journal.*
[2] The Friday Night Society was a gathering of the author's friends and colleagues, which met every two months or so for dinner, conversation, and the presentation of original parodies.

IV.
However, fearing we would bore them,
we sought seclusion in my den;
her songs grew faint, and to restore them,
I pushed my academic pen.
No luck. Oh, I was feeling tragic,
when suddenly, as if by magic,
she came and took me on a spin
to Pávlovsk, then turned west to Finland, toured all over Scandinavia,
hearing concerts here and there,
sang work's delight and love's despair,
then sójourned briefly in *Norvégia*,
and played the *cosmopolitaine*
as well as the *Varsovienne*.

V.

Then quitting northern Europe's cities,
with their successes and their woes,
in new-world Boston, fiddling ditties,
she played how a career grows
in new assignments and appointments,
drowned romantic disappointments,
forgot her fiddle's tenderer notes
for new professional anecdotes
and songs to working energetic;
impassioned suits she would disdain,
and settled in Jamaica Plain
to play the bachelor hermetic,
with eyes of wistful self-command,
baton and playing-cards in hand.

VI.

At Burgin's she has been sequestered
for five years now. He's said to shun
the opposite sex, by whom he's pestered,
preferring hands of bridge for fun.
Though he'll admit that he is lonely,
with each potential one-and-only,
he simply cannot get in stride,
or fears, perhaps, a loss of pride.
He often jokes to friends that he's a
great lover...of the game of whist,
and not a *real* misogynist,
occasionally sees Louisa,
who lives above him, and despairs
that just her photo stays downstairs.

VII.

He's used to bachelor existence,
its orderly disorder free
from the perturbing inconsistence
of "silly" femininity.
But wait! Who is that lovely creature,
as blessed by talent as by feature,
who just put down her instrument,
and heard from him a compliment,
he'd never pay to any student:
'I've never heard, it seems to me,
Tchaikovsky played more beautifully!'
Dear muse, who is this blonde intruder,
who won our Burgin's praise heartfelt?
'Why don't you know?! That's Ruth Posselt!

VIII.

the famed American violinist,
nedávno sdélavshaja furór[1]
in Soviet Russia, where she finished
her latest European tour.
March twenty fifth she'll be appearing
at Symphony, and slightly fearing
Koussevitzky's temper, she
called Burgin up, to ask if he
would hear her play, and maybe offer
suggestions. So, she came today,
and after he had heard her play,
he stood in admiration of her.'
'How interesting! Bravissimo!
What more about her do you know?'

IX.

Her pa, Émile, violist, preacher
of German values, had a fierce
attraction to an English teacher
and singer, Ida Lewis Pierce,
whose family lived in old New Bedford.
They married, settled down in Medford,
had Gladys, multiplied apace
with Molly, Marjorie, Emil, Grace,
Naomi, and the last of seven,
to join her sisterly quintet,
and soon her family's fame beget
with natural talent's lifting leaven,
was Ruth, a child prodigy,
who started violin at three.

---

[1] *nedávno sdélavshaja furór* = who recently made a sensation (Russian).

X.

How blessed the child who is childish,
blessed she who can on time mature,
who as a girl is free and wildish,
and then grows up to feel secure;
who, gifted, is not isolated,
and from her peers not alienated;
who wows the boys at sweet sixteen,
and marries happily her dream;
who wins at forty liberation
from children and the kitchen sink
to garden, work, or simply think;
who gets success and relaxation,
and hears through life how people choir:
Jane Doe's a woman I admire!

XI.

But it is sad to think of *Kinder*,
whose *Wunder* robs them of their youth,
incinerates their growth to cinder,
and cheats them of its booty—truth;
whose bright, prodigious aspirations,
whose ringing, glistening ovations,
are dulled by Wonder's double spoils:
excessive pampering and toils;
unbearable to see them shoulder
adult responsibilities,
while overwhelmed with *child-ese*;
eternal children growing older,
they tempt a doubly banal fate:
too much too soon, too little -late.

XII.

Ruth's childhood, or so I gather,
was torn by a parental rift:
her mother dreamed of fame; her father
would not commercialize her gift.
At six she made her first appearance
as *Child Wonder Violinist*,
at nine in Jordan Hall debuted,
in two years, Cárnegie ensued;
the raves made Ida more ambitious,
while Emil wished to hold Ruth back
from the exposing public track
which he considered meretricious;
he would not have his children roam,
and thought that girls should stay at home.

XIII.

Ruth found the bravos very pleasing,
and loved to play ("it was a game!"),
but feared enormously displeasing
her papa with her yen for fame.
She felt within a double longing,
desired uniqueness and belonging,
and strove to be unusual,
while wanting to be typical.
The split grew worse when in December,
of 'twenty four, her father died;
it left her feeling terrified,
and all her life she would remember,
exhaling guilt and fear of death,
his last, tormented gasps for breath.

XIV.

The next ten years brought vacillations
between the common and the extreme,
as Ruth received her educations
in striving for her double dream:
in school she read the usual titles,
on stage earned laurels for recitals;
in talent she soared up to best,
she fell in love, like all the rest;
in 'twenty nine was nominated
for *Typical American Girl*,[1]
then concertized around the world,
and recently the headlines stated
MISS POSSELT IS CROWNED QUEEN IN
AMERICA, ON VIOLIN.[2]

XV.

Well, that is all that I can tell you
about Posselt, until today,
but if you want to know her well, you
should really go and hear her play.
'I'd love to, but...' I answered sadly,
'I have no ticket.' 'Oh, I'll gladly
ask Burgin,' said my gracious muse,
'I'm almost sure he won't refuse,
and maybe we can sit together.'
'How very nice of you!' I praised.
'Thank you, but don't be amazed,
I know we've had some stormy weather,
but let's calm down, make up, and kiss,
I'm bored with solitary bliss.'

---

[1] *Boston Evening American*, April 2, 1929.
[2] *Boston Globe*, March 15, 1935.

Ruth Posselt, 1929.

XVI.

So, acting for our double pleasure,
my muse took me to symphony,
to hear Tchaikovsky, and to measure
RB's reaction to RP.
It seemed to us her playing captured
him from the start: he sat enraptured,
of every single note aware,
in spite of his impassive stare;
and when she started the cadenza,
he noticed how some bow-hairs broke,
waited for a paused up-stroke,
and, acting out of providence or
a sense she didn't want to stop,
got up, and deftly plucked them off.

XVII.

My muse gave me a nudge, and winking,
she smiled in her knowing way;
of course, I knew what she was thinking,
and as we clapped, she bent to say,
'Well, that was very nice and charming!'
I grinned, 'And typically disarming.'
'Exactly,' she affirmed, 'the start
of Richard Burgin's change of heart.'
As usual, I feigned protesting,
'Oh muse, I can't believe that's true!
For several years now, haven't you,
his friends, and he, all been attesting
that he's a bachelor confirmed?'
'Why yes! Confirmedly mistermed.'

XVIII.

'Muse! you're really too capricious!'
'What makes you say that? 'Tisn't so.'
'If not, then I'm a bit suspicious,
you know some things that I don't know.'
'Perhaps,' she cooed. 'Well, stop your teasing.
I thought you wanted to be pleasing?'
'Okay, okay, I'll tell you this -
the day she played for him, that Miss
Posselt, as she was leaving, mentioned
that she was looking for a place
to rehearse with piano. Burgin's face
lit up with smiles well-intentioned:
"You know, I have a great idea!
Why don't you come and practice here?"'

XIX.

I shrugged, 'That's just a friendly offer,
you know, collegiality...'
'*Don't* be dumb and play the scoffer!
I know when I've seen chemistry,
and thus, I'll make a small prediction,
which will brook no contradiction,
that B and P's bilabial fate
is binary, and they will mate.
However, there are circumstances,
obstacles which will take time
to overcome, but we won't rhyme;
there're always secrets in románces.
Though you, of course, I would indulge,
we'll skip the things I can't divulge.'

XX.

'Oh you're a mystifying creature,
a real provocateur in skirts!'
'Perhaps my most exciting feature,'
she purred, 'some mystery never hurts!'
'No doubt, but don't we have a duty
to truth?' 'Not if it mars the beauty
of our real-life romantic tale
with some dispensable detail.'
'But I don't want to be deceptive.'
'Really? Well, then give some clues;
your readers aren't all ingenues,
and those of them who are perceptive
will put together two and two;
the others shouldn't worry you.'

XXI.

I found my muse's view convincing,
but even more so, I must say,
my sense that you have been evincing
impatience at this long delay.
So onward, onward. In a blink we
move two years forward to Helsinki,
where B connected years before,
and P is now on concert tour.
She waits backstage. The concertmaster,
B's friend Hannikainnen, comes
bouqueted with red and yellow mums;
she reads the card, her heart beats faster:
'I know that you'll play beautifully,
in admiration, your R.B.'

XXII.

"I think those mums were the beginning
of our romance," she'd recollect,
as he would listen, silent, grinning,
in his machismo circumspect.
Indeed, though often separated,
their double longing escalated,
until, by nineteen thirty eight,
they were in love, and feeling great.
Theirs *was* most surely an attraction
of opposites, where each one feeds
the hunger of the other's needs
in satisfying interaction;
there was some dissonance, of course,
but harmony proved the stronger force.

XXIII.

Despite the difference in their ages,
their pasts, and personalities,
they'd both survived the harrowing stages
of growing up as prodigies;
despite the obvious disjunctions
between their backgrounds, by injunctions
of parents they had both been ruled -
in duteousness both were well-schooled;
despite the many oppositions,
both had suffered guilt from loss
of parents they revered as boss;
despite their different dispositions,
both had known the anguish of
a soul-tormenting youthful love.

XXIV.

Although each was a fine musician,
they were not rivals, but help-meets,
for she admired his erudition,
and he—her virtuosic feats.
True complements in education,
two tones in double intonation,
professionally you could not find
more unity of heart and mind;
and personally? Though I be slighting
the complex truth of the unheard,
to express attraction in one word,
I think that he found her exciting,
while she was fired up with vim
to make a married man of him.

XXV.

And toward marriage they were tending,
or should be, so the grapevine felt,
reporting Mr. B was spending
a lot of time with Miss Posselt.
Now quite adept at illustrating
the programme of American dating,
he'd drive her home to Medford, park,
and kiss the right girl in the dark;
and as these private moving pictures
became an ever later show,
the Boston matrons were not slow
to whisper their vicarious strictures:
'You know, dear, Ruthie's never in!'
'*Tsk*! could they be living...in sin?!'

XXVI.

But Ida had another worry
when seeing Ruth come in at night,
on tiptoe, in a fearful flurry
to hide the signs of her delight.
She understood Ruth's dreams and passion,
and did not want to quell or dash 'em,
but she'd by love and life been taught
the wisdom of the second thought,
especially concerning marriage;
she knew a woman needs must make
a choice, for dream's or passion's sake.
Though wedded bliss she'd not disparage,
she knew the burdens it begat,
and thought with Ruth she ought to chat.

XXVII.

'Is that you, Ruthie dear?' 'Why mother!'
Ruth flushed, 'are you still up? so late?'
'I couldn't sleep. It's such a bother,
but well, you know, I often wait. . .
until you're home.' 'Oh, ma, I'm sorry.
How I hate to cause you worry!'
'I know, but that's what mothers do.
When you're a mother, you will too.
But Ruth, if you don't feel too tired,'
'I'm wide awake.' '. . .I'd love to hear
about your evening.' 'Mama, dear,
I. . .I simply couldn't have desired
a better one, it's like a dream. . .'
she sighed, and said, with eyes agleam,

XXVIII.

'We're so in love. . .' 'And your ambitions?
remember how it was. . .before. . .'
'Oh ma! This time we're both musicians,
he understands me, and what's more,
he doesn't find my working stressful
and wants for me to be successful,
for when I have a big success,
it always gives him happiness.'
'Well. . .' Ida clasped her daughter's shoulder,
'I must admit, I love him too,
he's loving, soft, and kind to you,
I worry though, he's so. . .much older. . .
and that is something that could get,
well, that you later might regret.'

XXIX.

Ruth usually listened to her mother,
but this time felt that she was wrong;
her ear was captured by another,
less worried-for-the-future song.
He might be almost forty seven,
but Ruth was sure that seventh heaven
in 'forty was the only thing
the difference in their age would bring;
and to that bliss she soon was carried,
one dawn, when Richard spoke the word:
'These nights of ours are just absurd!
So don't you think we should get married?
I'm getting worried; if we keep
this up, we'll never get to sleep!'

XXX.

And so, that summer, naught regretting,
July the third, they tied the knot,
in an extraordinary setting,
or so, at least, I've always thought.
For several hours they'd been riding
the Berkshire country roads, deciding
that neither of them wished to cope
with ceremonies, but elope,
when Burgin, in some excitation,
by chance glanced at the dash: Alas!
the car was almost out of gas.
'I hope that we can find a station,'
he said, his heart about to sink.
'West Stockbridge has one, dear, I think.'

XXXI.

They found it, but it looked deserted,
until the owner, all in grease,
approached them: 'Help ya?' Burgin blurted,
in some relief, 'Yes, fill it, please.'
'You folks from round here?' 'No, just driving,'
they chimed in unison, and striving
to cover their excitedness.
He felt her tiny fingers' press,
and quickly turning to the owner,
'Is there. . .[he heard his own voice sound],
a. . .Justice of the Peace around?'
'You really are an out-of-towner,'
the main grinned imperceptibly,
'The Justice of the Peace is me.'

XXXII.

'Can we be married?' 'Sure, I'll only
just go wash up. Please step inside' (. . .)
'Now, you would like, which ceremony?'
'The fastest.' 'Fine. Well, who's the bride?'
'I'm Ruth Posselt.' 'Groom?' 'Richard Burgin.'
'Your occupations?' 'Both musicians. . .'
'And could I have the wedding bands?'
'We don't. . .' 'No matter, just join hands.'
Thus, in a station few in service
could ever have surpassed, they wed,
filled up with gas, and drove ahead,
in haste, but feeling much less nervous,
to celebrate their marriage with
the Speyers and the Hindemiths.

XXXIII.

'Muse, that *was* a charming story!'
'And every word of it was true.'
'It also was commendatory,
how in the end you managed to
effect a rather deft transition
to Hindemith, whose composition
involved the early married life
of Richard Burgin and his wife.'
'I thought that you'd appreciate that,'
she beamed with pride, 'but I need rest,
so don't you think it would be best
to have RB himself relate that?
You help him tell about his friend,
while I prepare our poem's end.'

XXXIV.

"Well, Hindemith was a terrific
personality, and he -
his knowledge being so prolific -
was very interesting to me.
I had extraordinary luck in
playing under him, conducting
his works, and then premiering in
the United states his Violin
Concerto.[1] Then, my wife took over
and played so beautifully that work,
that she performed it in New York,
with him, and everywhere, all over.
And yet, the way it came about
was very strange and roundabout.

XXXV.

"When he first came here, to this country,
in 'thirty nine, I think, although
he was reserved, we got quite friendly.
I used to argue with him. So
when I had got to know him better,
I said, once, 'Paul, I like your *Kammer-
musik*, and have been practicing. . .'
He said, 'Why bother studying
what isn't worth your time?' I felt he,
that this was strange. 'I don't agree.
I like this piece, but I don't see
why do you write so difficultly
for violin?' He said, again,
'Why should you bother with it then?'

---

[1] Richard Burgin gave the first American performance of the Hindemith Violin Concerto in Boston, April 19/20, 1940. Ruth Posselt played it in New York on January 9, 1941. (DLB)

XXXVI.

"I couldn't convince him, but a comment
I made did stop the argument.
I said, 'You know, Paul, from the moment
you have composed a piece, and sent
it off, you lose all jurisdiction,
because, without your benediction,
anyone can take it, and
has got the right to understand
it as he wants.' My little sermon
hit home; he said, 'Well, that is true.
You know, I'm going to send to you
a new concerto,' adding in German,
'wenige Noten, aber schön,'[1]
and therefore, easier to learn.

XXXVII.

" 'I'm sorry, though, the first performance
has been arranged, for Amsterdam.'
'I don't care about first performance;
just let me see it, if you can.'
Time passed. In May, when he was leaving
for Germany, still not receiving
this new concerto that's supposed
to be so *schön*, with fewer notes,
I thought, at first, 'well, that's another
of those nice things composers can,
well, promise, but. . .' Then I began
to think, 'Why really does he bother
to send it? He's published, after all.'
I went to him and told him, 'Paul!

---

[1] *wenige Noten, aber schön* = fewer notes, but beautiful (German).

XXXVIII.

" 'Why bother sending that concerto?
Who's your publisher?' 'Why, Schott.
But you can't buy that yet, I'm certain.'
'How come?' 'Because, you see, it's not
been printed.' 'Could you let me see a,
a manuscript?' I was so eager,
I loved his music long before
I had known him. He said, 'I'm sor-
ry, but, I simply haven't got one,
because it isn't written down.'
'How is that possible?' I frowned.
'It now is May, the first performance
for September has been set,
and you have not composed it yet?'

XXXIX.

" 'It is composed!' he answered, growing
a bit impatient, 'every note.
It's just not written, but I'm going
to Europe, as you know, by boat -
six days with nothing else to do, when
I'll write it down, and when I'm through, then
my publisher will be informed,
it will be printed and performed.'
And that's a fact, which I attested:
just like Bach and Mozart, he
could compose from memory.
Since I was always interested
in how composers can create,
he was, for me, a unique case.

XL.

"In fact, he finished, in Jamaica
Plain, the last three pages of
his Symphony in E-flat major,
in my den, at five o'clock...
I finally got, in February,
this new concerto. It *is* very
beautiful, and there are far,
far fewer notes. Thus his remark
was true, and also characteristic;
there were too many notes, you see,
in all his early works, but he,
as most composers do, got rid of
those barnacles that seem to grow
unneeded on the body, you know."

XLI.

'I hope, dear muse, by now you've rested,
and shall be able to expend
your energies, as you suggested,
to bring our story to an end.'
'Are you feeling awfully tired?'
'Not awfully, but my tale's expired,
so you take over now for me,
I know you'll play it beautifully.'
'I'll try my best!' she whispered, yawning,
got up, and rubbed her sleepy eyes.
'I've planned for you a small surprise,
which while I slept, my dreams were spawning,
and at the end, I'm sure, will give
new life to our long narrative.'

XLII.

Our newlyweds, their true love proving,
throughout the Berkshire summer thrive;
the fall of 'forty finds them moving
to Fifty-Seven Larchwood Drive,
in Cambridge, there, without the trouble
of dawn goodbyes, to start the double
concerto of their lives and hearts,
their contrapuntal minds and arts.
November's BSO Friends listen,
faces lit with major grins,
to Bach's d-minor violins,
and January premiers Piston,
with her great virtuosic feat,
conducted by his steady beat.[1]

XLIII.

Summer. Strolling through the arbor,
we spread our blanket in the sun
at Tanglewood, to hear her Barber,[2]
in August, nineteen forty one.
The season changes. In more sober
attire, chilled by late October,
we warm ourselves in Symphony Hall,
by her Dvorak held in thrall.
But on the heels of that ovation,
she leaves to tour the great mid-west,
while he, quite lonely, copes as best
he can with weeks of separation:
in work he muffles his dismay,
and writes her letters every day.

---

[1] Walter Piston composed his violin concerto for Miss Posselt in the summer of 1939. She played it with the BSO, Richard Burgin conducting, on Jan. 31/Feb.1, 1941.
[2] Ruth Posselt performed Samuel Barber's Violin Concerto at Tanglewood on August 16, and the Dvorak in Symphony Hall on Oct. 31/Nov. 1.

XLIV.

In 'forty two, he is promoted,
conducted to Associate,[1]
but we have dutifully noted
career's growth, and shan't relate
the ups and downs of each performance,
their aspirations and their torments;
there are other kinds of happiness
besides professional success.
Thus she, one night that fall, said 'Maybe,
my darling, something's missing in
our lives I love my violin,
but, would you like to have a...baby?'
His eyes beamed wide, with pleasure full,
'I think that would be wonderful.'

XLV.

So, was it by some intuition,
the fruit of prescient, shared romance,
or was it just the imposition
on Burgin's programming of Chance,
that January's symphoniana
was overtured by *Donna Diana*,
and dramatized the *Don* of Strauss,[2]
who sought so long the ideal spouse?
And by what chance was it constructed,
that on that venerable stage,
in March, still at a tender age,
as P performed and B conducted,
by both unseen, perhaps D heard
Dukelsky's *First* and Mahler's *Third*.[3]

---

[1] Richard Burgin began the 1942–43 season as Associate Conductor of the BSO.

[2] Burgin's program for Jan. 15/16, 1943 included Rezniček's *Overture to Donna Diana* and Strauss's *Don Quixote*.

[3] On March 19/20, 1943, Ruth Posselt gave the first performance of Dukelsky's Violin Concerto, and Richard Burgin concluded the program with the first Boston performance of the First Part of Mahler's Third Symphony.

XLVI.

Who knows what memories human beings
might form while still inside the womb?
what murky hearings, stirrings, seeings
might reach them in that liquid gloom?
Who knows if deeply-felt perceptions
might not recall some faint receptions
of major joy and minor blight
before we saw or heard the light?
I only know, *his* urge paternal,
so often stymied in his life,
has found fulfillment in his wife,
combining with *her* dream maternal,
and my *Life*'s ballad, *He* and *She*,
shall end with their creation—me.

XLVII.

On August third, in nervous torment,
our Ruth put down her violin,
unneeded in this first performance,
and left for Boston Lying-In.
After eighteen hours labor
(details of which I shan't belabor),
she caught a yell in spinal pause,
then rested up, and heard applause,
from Richard, Ida, friends, relations,
a deafening chorus of hurrays,
amid a flurry of bouquets,
with "heartiest congratulations"
esteeming her bravura's worth -
Diana Lewis Burgin's birth.

XLVIII.

The baby's home. Our Burgin, happy,
as if immersed in the sublime,
is feeding her, his shoulder nappy
all readied, as from time to time,
he puts the bottle down to hold her,
his left hand patting, to his shoulder...
But as he, smiling, waits to hear
the burp that's music to his ear,
we'll leave him, reader, for a while,
perhaps for good. Enough our whim
we've satisfied in following him
around the world. Let's share his smile
in having found a home at last -
the time for us to go is past!

XLIX.

Whoever you be, my reader, whether
hostile, friendly, false, or true,
right now, as friends, let's come together
to say goodbye. Whatever you
may seek in these eight motley chapters -
remembrances of stormy raptures,
a rest from life's imbroglio,
living pictures, or *bons mots*,
tortured syntax, or misspellings,
I hope that in this book you'll find,
for your distraction, for your mind,
your deepest yearnings, or your yellings -
some morsel which will satisfy,
and on that hope, we part: goodbye.

L.

Goodbye, my *muzykánt*[1] aspiring,
and you, my virtuoso mom,
and you, enlivening and tiring
unfinished *Life*. With you I've come
a long way in my versifying,
now fretting and now satisfying
my muse's worried, loving gaze.
So many, many gruelling days
have passed since that obscure November,
when, dreaming, I first caught the beat
of Burgin in Onegin feet,
and in the distance, I remember,
I stared, as in a crystal ball,
but could not see their end at all.

LI.

But, those friends, with whom it mattered
so much to share these stanzas first . . .
some remain, but others have scattered,
the Friday Night Club has dispersed.
Without it, most of this was written;
and he, with whom I was so smitten,
who formed my fatherly ideal. . .
it's hard to say goodbye for real.
And blessed the one who, growing older,
has learned that just the past is dead,
and smiling, eager, looks ahead,
a burping baby on his shoulder,
and can't foresee their parting strife
like me, with Burgin's half-lived *Life*.

---

[1] *muzykánt* = musician (Russian).

Richard Burgin and Donna Diana.

GLOSSARY OF NAMES

Arkády
: Bazarov's friend in Turgenev's *Fathers and Children*, who starts out as a fellow traveler of the nihilists (radicals), but ends up marrying and settling down to a life very much like his father's, only more productive, and financially secure.

Asya
: The heroine of Turgenev's story of the same name who is a victim of an unreciprocated first love.

Bazárov
: The gifted, but tragic, young "nihilist" hero of Turgenev's *Fathers and Children*. An example of the nineteenth-century "superfluous man" in Russian literature, he is tragically undermined by his unreciprocated passion for an attractive, but passionless widow, Odintsova.

Benois-Èfron
: Professor of piano at the Petersburg Conservatory before the 1917 Revolution. One of his prize-winning students, recipient of the Large Silver Medal in piano was a woman named Henrietta Rozenberg-Belskaia.

Connely, Willard
: 1888–1967. American educator and author, born in Atlantic City, N.J., married Louisa Fletcher (Tarkington) in 1915.

Dann, Elias
: Professor of music at Florida State University. In June, 1974 he did a lengthy taped interview with Richard Burgin at Burgin's home in Tallahassee.

Elman, Mischa
: 1881–1967. Russian-Jewish violinist and contemporary of Richard Burgin. Elman was one of the first in a long line of child prodigies who studied with Leopold Auer (1845–1930) at the St. Petersburg Conservatory. Elman's sensational debut in London in 1904 secured Auer's reputation as a

	pedagogue.
Epiphanius (the Wise)	A fifteenth-century Russian monk and hagiographer known for his ornamental style called "wordweaving."
Eugene	The poor-clerk hero of Pushkin's narrative poem, *The Bronze Horseman*, who loses his mind and runs crazed through the streets of St. Petersburg after a flood has killed his fiancée and ruined his modest dreams of happiness.
Fletcher, Louisa	1878–1957. American writer born in Indianapolis, graduate of Smith College (1900), married to Booth Tarkington (1902–1911), had one daughter, Nancy, from her second marriage (to W. Connely).
Gentle Creature	A story by Dostoevsky, published first in *Diary of a Writer*, 1876.
Gogolian zeroes	Nikolai Gogol (1809–52) was a renowned nineteenth-century Russian novelist, playwright and short-story writer. The heroes of his stories, many of which are set in St. Petersburg, tend to be mediocre, poor clerks and spiritual non-entities. The city exerts a magical, often demonic force on their lives.
Grevillius, Nils	Scandinavian conductor who frequently directed the Stockholm Symphony during Burgin's concertmastership there. Both Burgin and his first wife, Henriette, appeared as soloists under Grevillius's direction.
Hannikainnen	Finnish composer and violinist with whom Burgin became acquainted during the latter's years in Helsingfors.
Hérmann	The hero of Pushkin's short story, *The Queen of Spades*. Hérmann senses the city as a fateful force that leads him, while he is out walking one day, to the house of an old Countess, who, he has been told, possesses a magic card trick

	that could, if he gets it, win him a fortune at faro.
Ivánov, Víacheslav	1866–1949. A symbolist poet, Ivánov lived in an apartment in Petersburg known as the Tower. It was a leading, and very chic pre-revolutionary gathering place for Symbolist poets and other Silver Age notables in the arts.
Kajanus, Robert	1856–1933. Finnish composer and conductor.
Karamázov, Ivan	The tortured, self-lacerating intellectual rebel of Dostoevsky's *The Brothers Karamozov*.
Kavalérov	The hero of Yuri Olesha's novel, *Envy* (1927), who is obsessed with achieving old-fashioned, Western-style glory, and envies the achievements of the new Soviet men. Like many of his nineteenth-century forebears in Russian literature, the "superfluous men," Kavalerov fails to realize his potential both for lack of a social outlet congenial to his talents, and for weakness of character and will. He chooses to glory in his failure rather than to betray his ideal of glory with ordinary "bourgeois" success.
Koussevítzky, Serge	1874–1951. Russian conductor and double-bass virtuoso, later conductor of the Boston Symphony Orchestra (1924–49). During his pre-revolutionary conducting years in Russia, Koussevitzky had his own orchestra, which was based in Moscow. Whenever the orchestra performed in Petersburg and the demands of the work required additional players, as was the case with Scriabin's *Prometheus*, Koussevitzky would hire Conservatory students as extras.
Kreutzer Sonata	A late story (1889) by Tolstoy which contains one of the writer's most

GLOSSARY OF NAMES

	vociferous attacks against the sensuality of music and women, as well as conventional marriage, and the evils of Victorian sexual mores in general.
Lamb, Lady Caroline	The woman with whom Lord Byron had one of his most scandalous and passionate love affairs.
Lénsky	The secondary hero of Pushkin's *Eugene Onegin* who is killed (by his "friend" Eugene) in a duel which he fights to defend the honor of his first love, Olga.
Lótto, Iszýdor	1844–1936, Polish-Jewish violinist and composer who studied at the Paris Conservatory under Massart, concertized as a virtuoso, and retired from the stage because of a nervous breakdown. He became professor of violin at the Music Institute in Warsaw, but also taught privately.
Nastásya Filippovna	The tragic heroine and "beautiful lady" of Dostoevsky's *The Idiot*, she ends up being murdered by one of the two men who are madly and truly in love with her.
Nástenka	The young heroine of Dostoevsky's early story *White Nights* (1849). A spunky young woman, she lives in Petersburg with her grandmother, who is blind. To keep track of Nastenka's whereabouts, the grandmother pins her to her skirts.
Natásha, Pierre, and Prince Andréi	The three characters in Tolstoy's central love triangle in the novel. Natasha's first serious love is for Prince Andrei. It ends unhappily and contributes to Andrei's death wish. Pierre's first love for Hélène leads him into existential despair. Later he finds true happiness with Natasha.
Pechórin	The Byronic anti-hero and archetypal

Prince Andréi	"superfluous man" in Lermontov's novel, *A Hero of Our Time* (1840). One of the two main heroes of Tolstoy's *War and Peace*. He proposes to Natasha Rostóva, who accepts him but agrees to postpone their marriage for a year in deference to his father's wishes. The postponement turns out to be Andrei's undoing since Natasha grows restive in her belovèd's absence, begins to doubt his love, and almost is carried away, literally and figuratively, by another man, thus making the marriage impossible. Although Natasha acts imprudently, the onus is on Andrei, who, in Tolstoy's view, acts unnaturally in agreeing to postpone happiness and halt the flow of life.
Prince Mýshkin	The tragic hero and "positively beautiful man" of Dostoevsky's *The Idiot*, whose first love for Nastásya Filippovna is rejected by her with the most dire consequences for everyone involved, including Mýshkin's rival, Rogózhin, and his "second" love, Agláya.
Princess Parallelogram	Byron's sobriquet for his wife, Annabella Milbanke, because of her intelligence and interest in mathematics.
Oblomov (itizing)	A neologism of the author's [DLB] based on the character-type and attitudes of Oblomov, the hero of Goncharóv's novel by the same name, whose main "occupation" is indolent dreaming. Oblomov's opposite and close friend in the novel is a young, entrepreneurial Russianized German, Stolz, the incarnation of the energetic, striving, Faustian spirit.
Rubenstein, Antón	1829–94. Russian composer, pianist, and the first Rector, from 1860, of the Moscow Conservatory of Music. The

GLOSSARY OF NAMES

	Petersburg Conservatory was established two years later.
Salieri, Antonio	The secondary composer and legendary poisoner of his contemporary, Mozart, as interpreted by Pushkin in his "little tragedy," *Mozart and Salieri*.
Sánin	The hero and title of a decadent novel by the otherwise little known Russian writer, Artsybashev, which caused a scandal when it first appeared in 1907 because of its erotic theme.
Schnéevoigt, Georg	1872–1947. Finnish conductor and impressario, founder of the Helsingfors City Orchestra (1912), director of the Stockholm Konsertförening (1915–24), and founder of the Oslo Symphony (in 1919).
Scriabin, Alexander	1878–1915. Russian composer and virtuoso pianist. By the time of his death Scriabin had achieved mythic status in Russian intellectual and artistic circles as the self-proclaimed "musical messiah" of the Silver Age. Strongly influenced by Wagner and the idea of the *Gesamftkunstwerke*, he strove for musical compositions that would unify all the arts.
Silver Age	The name applied to the turn-of-the-century symbolist/modernist period in Russian culture from 1893 to the Revolution of 1917.
Silvio	The pseudo-romantic, envious, and vengeance-obsessed hero of Pushkin's short story, *The Shot*.
Sitt, Anton	A violinist in the Helsingfors Orchestra and Burgin's chair-companion when he first joined that orchestra in 1912.
Solomon, Maynard	A recent biographer of Beethoven who is credited with discovering the identity of the composer's "Immortal Beloved."

Stenhammar, K. W.	1871–1917. Swedish composer, pianist, and conductor whose series of six quartets was considered unique in Swedish music at the time they were composed.
superfluous man	The name applied in literary criticism to the main type of nineteenth-century Russian literary hero. The superfluous man reflects Russian authors' fascination with one aspect of Shakespeare's Hamlet, who was perhaps the most influential of his tragic heroes in Russian literature and culture.
Tatíana	The heroine of Pushkin's *Eugene Onegin* who is roundly rejected by Eugene in her love for him, but recoups and in the end rejects him when he finally wants her. After Eugene leaves the country, having killed his friend Lensky in a duel, Tatiana visits his estate, and looks through the books in his library, trying to penetrate his character.
Tiutchev, Fyodor	1803–73. A major nineteenth-century Russian Romantic poet.
Tolstoy's arch-purity	The puritanical tendency in Russian literary culture reached its apogee in the late dogmatic preachments of Tolstoy, who died in early November, 1910, and whose obsession with purity, together with his well-known philosophy of non-resistance to evil by force were tremendously influential on a large segment of Russian educated youth.
Volpe, Arnold	1869–1940. Russian-American conductor. In 1902 he founded the Young Men's Symphony Orchestra of New York and also conducted a group called the Volpe Symphony Orchestra (1904–14).
Vrónsky and Anna	The star-cross'd lovers of Tolstoy's novel, *Anna Karenina*.
Warsaw Philharmonic	This orchestra, founded in 1901 and

	called "the pride of Poland," gave an annual summer festival at Riga during the pre-war years.
White Nights	Dostoevsky's early story which uses the magical atmosphere of the white nights in Petersburg to orchestrate the bittersweet romance between the hero, a dreamer, and his first love, Nastenka.
World of Art	A movement in the visual arts led by the artist, Benois, which began in Petersburg in the late 1890s. The members of this group, like Scriabin in music, sought artistic expression that was cosmopolitan and aimed at synthesis of various art forms.
Zimbalist, Efrem	Born 1889. Russian violinist and student of Auer, active in America. He made his debut in 1907.

SOURCE MATERIALS

I. BOOKS CONSULTED

Aldrich, Richard. *Concert Life in New York 1902–1923* (New York, 1941).
Alexeyev, A. D. *Russkie pianisti* (Moscow, 1948).
Auer, Leopold. *My Long Life in Music* (New York, 1923).
Camner, James, ed. *The Great Instrumentalists in Historic Photographs* (Dover, New York, 1980).
Connely, Louisa. *The Land of Beginning Again* (Boston, 1921).
Ganina, M., ed. *A. Glazunov: pis'ma, stat'i, vospominanija* (Moscow, 1958).
Golebiowski, M. *Filharmonia w Warszawie 1901–76* (Krakow, 1976).
Johnson, H. E. *Sibelius* (London, 1959).
Jusefovich. *David Oistrakh* (Cassel, London, 1979).
Kupferberg, Harold. *Tanglewood* (McGraw Hill, 1976).
Kowalski, Jozef. *Trudne lata* (Warsaw, 1966).
Kremlev, Yu. *Leningradskaja gosudarstvennaja konservatorija 1861–1937* (Moscow, 1938).
Levas, Santeri. *Jarven paan mestari*, Vol. 2 (Helsinki, 1960).
Malinowski, Marian. *PPS-Lewicz 1926–31 (Warsaw, 1963) Geneza PPR* (Warsaw, 1975).
Puzyrevskii. *Ocherk piatdesiatiletiia deyatel'nosti S. P. konservatorii* (Petrograd, 1912).
Raaben, Lev. *Leopol'd Auer* (Moscow, 1962).
Ringbom, Nils E. *Helsingfors orkesterföretag 1881–1921* (Helsinki, 1932).
Rudakova, ed. *A. N. Scriabin* (Moscow, 1979).
Smith, Moses. *Koussevitzky* (New York, 1947).
Unger-Hamilton, C., ed. *The Music Makers* (New York, 1979).

II. NEWSPAPERS

A. Obituaries of Richard Burgin

Boston Globe, April 30, 1981
Boston Herald American, April 30, 1981
The St. Petersburg Times, April 30, 1981
The Berkshire Eagle, April 30, 1981
New York Times, May 1, 1981
Brookline Chronical Citizen, May 21, 1981
BSO Newsletter, Summer, 1981
International Musician, October, 1981

B. Articles

BSO Press Office, *Fact Sheet* on Richard Burgin
Downes, Olin, Interview with Richard Burgin, *Boston Post*, October 1, 1920
Dyer, Richard, "Colleagues pay tribute to a musical giant,"

Boston Sunday Globe, May 10, 1981

Ehlers, Sabine, "Music Is His World," *Tampa Tribune*, October 1, 1971

Good Listening, "First Chair: Richard Burgin," Vol. 2, No. 4, September, 1953

Harris, McLaren, "Professor Burgin Chats On Music," *Boston Sunday Herald*, November 6, 1966

Sabin, Robert, "Richard Burgin, Veteran In Two Careers," *Musical American*, 1962

Taylor, Robert, "A Seeker Of Truth," *Boston Globe*, June 4, 1981

C. Reviews of Concerts

1. Russian

Zapadnyj golos (Warsaw), December 23, 1904
Golos Warshavy (Warsaw), December 29, 1904
Warshavskii dnevnik (Warsaw), December 30, 1904
Russkaja muzykal' naja gazeta: 1910 (No. 20–21); 1912 (No. 21–22); 1914 (No. 17–18)

2. Swedish

Dagens Nyheter, December 11, 1916
Nya Dagligt Allehande: October 6, 1916; March 2, 1917; November 23, 1917; March 5, 1918; January 10, 1919
Stockholms Tidningen: October 6, 1916; October 30, 1916; December 11, 1916; March 2, 1917; November 23, 1917; January 25, 1919; April 7, 1919
Svenska Dagbladet: October 6, 1916; December 11, 1916; October 5, 1917; November 23, 1917; January 10, 1919; January 24, 1919

3. American

New York Sun: November 22, 1907; March 16, 1923
New York Times: March 17, 1907; April 14, 1907; April 15, 1907; November 22, 1907; March 20, 1921; March 6, 1923; March 16, 1923; February 16, 1947; February 10, 1948; February 22, 1948; January 13, 1949; February 18, 1951; January 14, 1954; January 10, 1957; January 13, 1957; January 28, 1962; November 18, 1966
New York Herald, March 20, 1921
New York Tribune, March 20, 1921
Brooklyn Standard Union: March 17, 1923; April 9, 1927
Brooklyn Times: April 9, 1927; March 9, 1929

Boston Advertiser, March 19, 1927
Boston American: December 18, 1920; March 24, 1923; March 2, 1929
Boston Globe: December 18, 1920; April 11, 1922; March 19, 1927; March 2, 1929; February 1, 1941
Boston Herald: December 18, 1920; March 24, 1923; March 19, 1927; February 1, 1941
Boston Transcript: December 17, 1920; December 18, 1920; April 11, 1922; February 9, 1923; March 2, 1929; March 15, 1929
Boston Traveler, March 2, 1929
Christian Science Monitor: December 18, 1920; April 11, 1922; March 2, 1929; February 1, 1941
Providence Journal, January 26, 1921

III. UNPUBLISHED MATERIALS

1. Interviews

Professor Elias Dann of Florida State University with Richard Burgin in May–June, 1974.

Professor Diana Burgin with Maria Wierna (Burgin), former Minister of Foreign Affairs for Socialist Countries in Poland and widow of Juliusz Burgin, in August, 1981.

Mr. George Lawlor (Research Assistant) with Professor Ernst Törnquist, former member of the Burgin String Quartet in Stockholm (1916–19), in June, 1981.

Professor Diana Burgin with Nora Burgin, daughter of Leo Burgin, Richard Burgin's uncle, in the spring, 1981.

Professor Diana Burgin with Maria Morawski, daughter of Lily Burgin, Richard Burgin's sister, in August, 1981.

2. Letters

To Richard Burgin from various musicians, 1902 to 1966.
To Diana Burgin from Richard Burgin.
To Diana Burgin from Maria Morawski (see above), concerning Burgin family history.

Other Books From Slavica

Ronelle Alexander: *The Structure of Vasko Popa's Poetry*, 196 p., 1986 (ISBN: 0-89357-149-0), (UCLA Slavic Studies, Volume 14).

American Contributions to the Tenth International Congress of Slavists, Sofia, September, 1988, Linguistics, edited by Alexander M. Schenker, 439 p., 1988 (ISBN: 0-89357-190-3)

American Contributions to the Tenth International Congress of Slavists, Sofia, September, 1988, Literature, edited by Jane Gary Harris, 433 p., 1988 (ISBN: 0-89357-191-1)

American Contributions to the Ninth International Congress of Slavists (Kiev 1983) *Vol. 1: Linguistics,* ed. by Michael S. Flier, 381 p., 1983 (ISBN: 0-89357-112-1).

American Contributions to the Ninth International Congress of Slavists, (Kiev 1983) *Vol. 2: Literature, Poetics, History,* ed. by Paul Debreczeny, 400 p., 1983 (ISBN: 0-89357-113-X).

American Contributions to the Eighth International Congress of Slavists (Zagreb and Ljubljana, Sept. 3-9, 1978), *Vol 1: Linguistics and Poetics,* ed. by Henrik Birnbaum, 818 p., 1978 (ISBN: 0-89357-126-1).

American Contributions to the Eighth International Congress of Slavists (Zagreb and Ljubljana, Sept. 3-9, 1978) *Vol. 2: Literature,* ed. by Victor Terras, 799 p., 1978 (ISBN: 0-89357-047-8).

Patricia M. Arant: *Russian for Reading,* 214 p., 1981 (ISBN: 0-89357-086-9).

Howard I. Aronson: *Georgian: A Reading Grammar,* 526 p., 1982 (ISBN: 0-89357-100-8).

James E. Augerot and Florin D. Popescu: *Modern Romanian,* xiv + 330 p., 1983 (ISBN: 0-89357-124-5).

Adele Marie Barker: *The Mother Syndrome in the Russian Folk Imagination,* 180 p., 1986 (ISBN: 0-89357-160-1).

R. P. Bartlett, A. G. Cross, and Karen Rasmussen, eds.: *Russia and the World of the Eighteenth Century,* viii + 684 p., 1988 (ISBN: 0-89357-186-5).

John D. Basil: *The Mensheviks in the Revolution of 1917,* 220 p., 1984 (ISBN: 0-89357-109-1).

Other Books From Slavica

Henrik Birnbaum: *Lord Novgorod the Great Part One: The Historical Background,* 170 p., 1981 (ISBN: 0-89357-088-5) (UCLA Slavic Studies, Volume 2).

Henrik Birnbaum & Thomas Eekman, eds.: *Fiction and Drama in Eastern and Southeastern Europe: Evolution and Experiment in the Postwar Period,* ix + 463 p., 1980 (ISBN: 0-89357-064-8) (UCLA Slavic Studies, Volume 1).

Henrik Birnbaum and Peter T. Merrill: *Recent Advances in the Reconstruction of Common Slavic (1971-1982),* vi + 141 p., 1985 (ISBN: 0-89357-116-4).

Marianna D. Birnbaum: *Humanists in a Shattered World: Croatian and Hungarian Latinity in the Sixteenth Century,* 456 p., 1986 (ISBN: 0-89357-155-5). (UCLA Slavic Studies, Volume 15).

Feliks J. Bister and Herbert Kuhner, eds.: *Carinthian Slovenian Poetry,* 216 p., 1984 (ISBN: 3-85013-029-0).

Karen L. Black, ed.: *A Biobibliographical Handbook of Bulgarian Authors,* 347 p., 1982 (ISBN: 0-89357-091-5).

Marianna Bogojavlensky: *Russian Review Grammar,* xviii + 450 p., 1982 (ISBN: 0-89357-096-6).

Rodica C. Boțoman, Donald E. Corbin, E. Garrison Walters: *Îmi Place Limba Română/A Romanian Reader,* 199 p., 1982 (ISBN: 0-89357-087-7).

Richard D. Brecht and James S. Levine, eds: *Case in Slavic,* 467 p., 1986 (ISBN: 0-89357-166-0).

Gary L. Browning: *Workbook to Russian Root List,* 85 p., 1985 (ISBN: 0-89357-114-8).

R. L. Busch: *Humor in the Major Novels of Dostoevsky,* 168 p., 1987 (ISBN: 0-89357-176-8).

Catherine V. Chvany and Richard D. Brecht, eds.: *Morphosyntax in Slavic,* v + 316 p., 1980 (ISBN: 0-89357-070-2).

Jozef Cíger-Hronský: *Jozef Mak* (a novel), translated from Slovak by Andrew Cincura, Afterword by Peter Petro, 232 p., 1985 (ISBN: 0-89357-129-6).

Frederick Columbus: *Introductory Workbook in Historical Phonology,* 39 p., 1974 (ISBN: 0-89357-018-4).

Other Books From Slavica

Julian W. Connolly and Sonia I. Ketchian, eds.: *Studies in Russian Literature in Honor of Vsevolod Setchkarev*, 288 p. 1987 (ISBN: 0-89357-174-1).

Gary Cox: *Tyrant and Victim in Dostoevsky*, 119 p., 1984 (ISBN: 0-89357-125-3).

Anna Lisa Crone and Catherine V. Chvany, eds.: *New Studies in Russian Language and Literature*, 302 p., 1987 (ISBN: 0-89357-168-7).

R. G. A. de Bray: *Guide to the South Slavonic Languages (Guide to the Slavonic Languages, Third Edition, Revised and Expanded, Part 1)*, 399 p., 1980 (ISBN: 0-89357-060-5).

Carolina De Maegd-Soëp: *Chekhov and Women: Women in the Life and Work of Chekhov*, 373 p., 1987 (ISBN: 0-89357-175-X).

Bruce L. Derwing and Tom M. S. Priestly: *Reading Rules for Russian: A Systematic Approach to Russian Spelling and Pronunciation, with Notes on Dialectal and Stylistic Variation*, vi + 247 p., 1980 (ISBN: 0-89357-066-4).

Dorothy Disterheft: *The Syntactic Development of the Infinitive in Indo-European*, 220 p., 1980 (ISBN: 0-89357-058-3).

Thomas Eekman and Dean S. Worth, eds.: *Russian Poetics* Proceedings of the International Colloquium at UCLA, September 22-26, 1975, 544 p., 1983 (ISBN: 0-89357-101-6) (UCLA Slavic Studies, Volume 4).

James S. Elliott: *Russian for Trade Negotiations with the USSR*, 356 p., 1981 (ISBN: 0-89357-084-2).

Ralph Carter Elwood, ed.: *Reconsiderations on the Russian Revolution*, x + 278 p., 1976 (ISBN: 0-89357-035-4).

Michael S. Flier and Richard D. Brecht, eds.: *Issues in Russian Morphosyntax*, 208 p., 1985 (ISBN: 0-89357-139-3) (UCLA Slavic Studies, Volume 10).

Michael S. Flier and Alan Timberlake, eds: *The Scope of Slavic Aspect*, 295 p., 1985 (ISBN: 0-89357-150-4). (UCLA Slavic Studies, Volume 12).

Other Books From Slavica

John Miles Foley, ed.: *Comparative Research on Oral Traditions: A Memorial for Milman Parry*, 597 p., 1987 (ISBN: 0-89357-173-3).

John M. Foley, ed.: *Oral Traditional Literature A Festschrift for Albert Bates Lord*, 461 p., 1981 (ISBN: 0-89357-073-7).

Diana Greene: *Insidious Intent: An Interpretation of Fedor Sologub's The Petty Demon*, 140 p., 1986 (ISBN: 0-89357-158-X).

Charles E. Gribble, ed.: *Medieval Slavic Texts, Vol. 1, Old and Middle Russian Texts*, 320 p., 1973 (ISBN: 0-89357-011-7).

Charles E. Gribble: *Reading Bulgarian Through Russian*, 182 p., 1987 (ISBN: 0-89357-106-7).

Charles E. Gribble: *Russian Root List with a Sketch of Word Formation, Second Edition*, 62 p., 1982 (ISBN: 0-89357-052-4).

Charles E. Gribble: *A Short Dictionary of 18th-Century Russian*/Словарик Русского Языка 18-го Века, 103 p., 1976 (ISBN: 0-89357-172-5).

Charles E. Gribble, ed.: *Studies Presented to Professor Roman Jakobson by His Students*, 333 p. (7 x 10" format), 1968, (ISBN: 0-89357-000-1).

George J. Gutsche and Lauren G. Leighton, eds.: *New Perspectives on Nineteenth-Century Russian Prose*, 146 p., 1982 (ISBN: 0-89357-094-X).

Morris Halle, ed.: *Roman Jakobson: What He Taught Us*, 94 p., 1983 (ISBN: 0-89357-118-0). (Free as supplement to issue No. 27 of *IJSLP*, otherwise available as a separate book.)

Charles J. Halperin: *The Tatar Yoke*, 231 p., 1986 (ISBN: 0-89357-161-X).

William S. Hamilton: *Introduction to Russian Phonology and Word Structure*, 187 p., 1980 (ISBN: 0-89357-063-X).

Pierre R. Hart: *G. R. Derzhavin: A Poet's Progress*, iv + 164 p., 1978 (ISBN: 0-89357-054-0).

Michael Heim: *Contemporary Czech*, 271 p., 1982 (ISBN: 0-89357-098-2) (UCLA Slavic Studies, Volume 3).

Other Books From Slavica

Michael Heim, Zlata Meyerstein, and Dean Worth: *Readings in Czech*, 147 p., 1985 (ISBN: 0-89357-154-7). (UCLA Slavic Studies, Volume 13).

Warren H. Held, Jr., William R. Schmalstieg, and Janet E. Gertz: *Beginning Hittite*, ix + 218 p., 1988 (ISBN: 0-89357-184-9).

M. Hubenova & others: *A Course in Modern Bulgarian, Part 1*, viii + 303 p., 1983 (ISBN: 0-89357-104-0); *Part 2*, ix + 303 p., 1983 (ISBN: 0-89357-105-9).

Martin E. Huld: *Basic Albanian Etymologies*, x + 213 p., 1984 (ISBN: 0-89357-135-0).

Charles Isenberg: *Substantial Proofs of Being: Osip Mandelstam's Literary Prose*, 179 p., 1987 (ISBN: 0-89357-169-5).

Roman Jakobson, with the assistance of Kathy Santilli: *Brain and Language Cerebral Hemispheres and Linguistic Structure in Mutual Light*, 48 p., 1980 (ISBN: 0-89357-068-0). (New York University Slavic Papers, Interdisciplinary Series, Volume IV)

Donald K. Jarvis and Elena D. Lifshitz: *Viewpoints: A Listening and Conversation Course in Russian, Third Edition*, iv + 66 p., 1985 (ISBN: 0-89357-152-0); *Instructor's Manual*, v + 37 p., (ISBN: 0-89357-153-9).

Leslie A. Johnson: *The Experience of Time in Crime and Punishment*, 146 p., 1985 (ISBN: 0-89357-142-3).

Raina Katzarova-Kukudova and Kiril Djenev: *Bulgarian Folk Dances*, 174 p., numerous illustrations, 1976 (ISBN: 0-89357-029-X).

Emily R. Klenin: *Animacy in Russian: A New Interpretation*, 139 p., 1983 (ISBN: 0-89357-115-6). (UCLA Slavic Studies, Volume 6)

Andrej Kodjak, Krystyna Pomorska, and Kiril Taranovsky, eds.: *Alexander Puškin Symposium II*, 131 p., 1980 (ISBN: 0-89357-067-2) (New York University Slavic Papers, Volume III).

Andrej Kodjak, Krystyna Pomorska, Stephen Rudy, eds.: *Myth in Literature*, 207 p., 1985 (ISBN: 0-89357-137-7) (New York University Slavic Papers, Volume V).

Andrej Kodjak: *Pushkin's I. P. Belkin*, 112 p., 1979 (ISBN: 0-89357-057-5).

Other Books From Slavica

Andrej Kodjak, Michael J. Connolly, Krystyna Pomorska, eds.: *Structural Analysis of Narrative Texts (Conference Papers)*, 203 p., 1980 (ISBN: 0-89357-071-0) (New York University Slavic Papers, Volume II).

Demetrius J. Koubourlis, ed.: *Topics in Slavic Phonology*, vii + 270 p., 1974 (ISBN: 0-89357-017-6).

Ronald D. LeBlanc: *The Russianization of Gil Blas: A Study in Literary Appropriation*, 292 p. 1986 (ISBN: 0-89357-159-8).

Richard L. Leed, Alexander D. Nakhimovsky, and Alice S. Nakhimovsky: *Beginning Russian, Vol. 1*, xiv + 426 p., 1981 (ISBN: 0-89357-077-X); *Vol. 2*, viii + 339 p., 1982 (ISBN: 0-89357-078-8); *Teacher's Manual*, 45 p., 1981 (ISBN: 0-89357-079-6).

Richard L. Leed and Slava Paperno: *5000 Russian Words With All Their Inflected Forms: A Russian-English Dictionary*, xiv + 322 p., 1987 (ISBN: 0-89357-170-9).

Edgar H. Lehrman: *A Handbook to Eighty-Six of Chekhov's Stories in Russian*, 327 p., 1985 (ISBN: 0-89357-151-2).

Lauren Leighton, ed.: *Studies in Honor of Xenia Gąsiorowska*, 191 p., 1983 (ISBN: 0-89357-102-4).

R. L. Lencek: *The Structure and History of the Slovene Language*, 365 p., 1982 (ISBN: 0-89357-099-0).

Jules F. Levin and Peter D. Haikalis, with Anatole A. Forostenko: *Reading Modern Russian*, vi + 321 p., 1979 (ISBN: 0-89357-059-1).

Maurice I. Levin: *Russian Declension and Conjugation:* A Structural Description with Exercises, x + 159 p., 1978 (ISBN: 0-89357-048-6).

Alexander Lipson: *A Russian Course. Part 1*, ix + 338 p., 1981 (ISBN: 0-89357-080-X); *Part 2*, 343 p., 1981 (ISBN: 0-89357-081-8); *Part 3*, iv + 105 p., 1981 (ISBN: 0-89357-082-6); *Teacher's Manual* by Stephen J. Molinsky (who also assisted in the writing of Parts 1 and 2), 222 p., 1981 (ISBN: 0-89357-083-4).

Yvonne R. Lockwood: *Text and Context Folksong in a Bosnian Muslim Village*, 220 p., 1983 (ISBN: 0-89357-120-2).

Other Books From Slavica

Sophia Lubensky & Donald K. Jarvis, eds.: *Teaching, Learning, Acquiring Russian*, viii + 415 p., 1984 (ISBN: 0-89357-134-2).

Horace G. Lunt: *Fundamentals of Russian*, xiv + 402 p., reprint, 1982 (ISBN: 0-89357-097-4).

Paul Macura: *Russian-English Botanical Dictionary*, 678 p., 1982 (ISBN: 0-89357-092-3).

Thomas G. Magner, ed.: *Slavic Linguistics and Language Teaching*, x + 309 p., 1976 (ISBN: 0-89357-037-0).

Vladimir Markov and Dean S. Worth, eds.: *From Los Angeles to Kiev Papers on the Occasion of the Ninth International Congress of Slavists*, 250 p., 1983 (ISBN: 0-89357-119-9) (UCLA Slavic Studies, Volume 7).

Mateja Matejić and Dragan Milivojević: *An Anthology of Medieval Serbian Literature in English*, 205 p., 1978 (ISBN: 0-89357-055-9).

Peter J. Mayo: *The Morphology of Aspect in Seventeenth-Century Russian (Based on Texts of the Smutnoe Vremja)*, xi + 234 p., 1985 (ISBN: 0-89357-145-8).

Gordon M. Messing: *A Glossary of Greek Romany As Spoken in Agia Varvara (Athens)*, 175 p., 1988 (ISBN: 0-89357-187-3).

Vasa D. Mihailovich and Mateja Matejic: *A Comprehensive Bibliography of Yugoslav Literature in English, 1593-1980*, xii + 586 p., 1984 (ISBN: 0-89357-136-9).

Edward Mozejko, ed.: *Vasiliy Pavlovich Aksenov: A Writer in Quest of Himself*, 272 p., 1986 (ISBN: 0-89357-141-5).

Edward Możejko: *Yordan Yovkov*, 117 p., 1984 (ISBN: 0-89357-117-2).

Alexander D. Nakhimovsky and Richard L. Leed: *Advanced Russian, Second Edition, Revised*, vii + 262 p., 1987 (ISBN: 0-89357-178-4).

The Comprehensive Russian Grammar of A. A. Barsov/ Обстоятельная грамматика А. А. Барсова, Critical Edition by Lawrence W. Newman, lxxxvi + 382 p., 1980 (ISBN: 0-89357-072-9).

Felix J. Oinas: *Essays on Russian Folklore and Mythology*, 183 p., 1985, (ISBN: 0-89357-148-2).

Other Books From Slavica

Hongor Oulanoff: *The Prose Fiction of Veniamin Kaverin*, v + 203 p., 1976 (ISBN: 0-89357-032-X).

Temira Pachmuss: *Russian Literature in the Baltic between the World Wars*, 448 p., 1988 (ISBN: 0-89357-181-4).

Lora Paperno: *Getting Around Town in Russian: Situational Dialogs*, English translation and photographs by Richard D. Sylvester, 123 p., 1987 (ISBN: 0-89357-171-7).

Slava Paperno, Alexander D. Nakhimovsky, Alice S. Nakhimovsky, and Richard L. Leed: *Intermediate Russian: The Twelve Chairs*, 326 p., 1985, (ISBN: 0-89357-144-X).

Ruth L. Pearce: *Russian For Expository Prose, Vol. 1 Introductory Course*, 413 p., 1983 (ISBN: 0-89357-121-0); *Vol. 2 Advanced Course*, 255 p., 1983 (ISBN: 0-89357-122-9).

Gerald Pirog: *Aleksandr Blok's* Итальянские Стихи *Confrontation and Disillusionment*, 219 p., 1983 (ISBN: 0-89357-095-8).

Stanley J. Rabinowitz: *Sologub's Literary Children: Keys to a Symbolist's Prose*, 176 p., 1980 (ISBN: 0-89357-069-9).

Gilbert C. Rappaport: *Grammatical Function and Syntactic Structure: The Adverbial Participle of Russian*, 218 p., 1984 (ISBN: 0-89357-133-4) (UCLA Slavic Studies, Volume 9).

David F. Robinson: *Lithuanian Reverse Dictionary*, ix + 209 p., 1976 (ISBN: 0-89357-034-6).

Don K. Rowney & G. Edward Orchard, eds.: *Russian and Slavic History*, viii + 303 p., 1977 (ISBN: 0-89357-036-2).

Catherine Rudin: *Aspects of Bulgarian Syntax: Complementizers and WH Constructions*, iv + 232 p., 1986, (ISBN: 0-89357-156-3).

Gerald J. Sabo, S.J., ed.: *Valaská Škola, by Hugolin Gavlovič, with a linguistic sketch by Ľubomír Ďurovič*, 730 p., 1988 (ISBN: 0-89357-179-2).

Ernest A. Scatton: *Bulgarian Phonology*, xii + 224 p., 1975 (reprint: 1983) (ISBN: 0-89357-103-2).

Ernest A. Scatton: *A Reference Grammar of Modern Bulgarian*, 448 p., 1984 (ISBN: 0-89357-123-7).

William R. Schmalstieg: *Introduction to Old Church Slavic, second edition*, 314 p., 1983 (ISBN: 0-89357-107-5).

Other Books From Slavica

William R. Schmalstieg: *A Lithuanian Historical Syntax*, xi + 412 p., 1988 (ISBN: 0-89357-185-7).

R. D. Schupbach: *Lexical Specialization in Russian,* 102 p., 1984 (ISBN: 0-89357-128-8) (UCLA Slavic Studies, Volume 8).

Peter Seyffert: *Soviet Literary Structuralism: Background Debate Issues,* 378 p., 1985 (ISBN: 0-89357-140-7).

Kot K. Shangriladze and Erica W. Townsend, eds.: Papers for the V. Congress of Southeast European Studies (Belgrade, September 1984), 382 p., 1984 (ISBN: 0-89357-138-5).

Michael Shapiro: *Aspects of Russian Morphology, A Semiotic Investigation,* 62 p. (7 x 10" format), 1969 (ISBN: 0-89357-004-4).

J. Thomas Shaw: *Pushkin A Concordance to the Poetry,* 2 volumes, 1310 pages total, 1985 (ISBN: 0-89357-130-X for the set).

Efraim Sicher: *Style and Structure in the Prose of Isaak Babel',* 169 p., 1986 (ISBN: 0-89357-163-6).

Mark S. Simpson: *The Russian Gothic Novel and its British Antecedents,* 112 p., 1986 (ISBN: 0-89357-162-8).

Greta N. Slobin, ed.: *Aleksej Remizov: Approaches to a Protean Writer,* 286 p., 1987 (ISBN: 0-89357-167-9).

Theofanis G. Stavrou and Peter R. Weisensel: *Russian Travelers to the Christian East from the Twelfth to the Twentieth Century,* L + 925 p., 1985, (ISBN: 0-89357-157-1).

Gerald Stone and Dean S. Worth, eds.: *The Formation of the Slavonic Literary Languages, Proceedings of a Conference Held in Memory of Robert Auty and Anne Pennington at Oxford 6-11 July 1981,* 269 p., 1985 (ISBN: 0-89357-143-1) (UCLA Slavic Studies, Volume 11).

Roland Sussex and J. C. Eade, eds.: *Culture and Nationalism in Nineteenth-Century Eastern Europe,* 158 p., 1985 (ISBN: 0-89357-146-6).

Oscar E. Swan: *First Year Polish, second edition, revised and expanded,* 354 p., 1983 (ISBN: 0-89357-108-3).

Oscar E. Swan: *Intermediate Polish,* 370 p., 1986 (ISBN: 0-89357-165-2).

Other Books From Slavica

Charles E. Townsend: *Continuing With Russian*, xxi + 426 p., 1981 (ISBN: 0-89357-085-0).

Charles E. Townsend and Veronica N. Dolenko: *Instructor's Manual to Accompany Continuing With Russian*, 39 p., 1987 (ISBN: 0-89357-177-6).

Charles E. Townsend: *Czech Through Russian*, viii + 263 p., 1981 (ISBN: 0-89357-089-3).

Charles E. Townsend: *The Memoirs of Princess Natal'ja Borisovna Dolgorukaja*, viii + 146 p., 1977 (ISBN: 0-89357-044-3).

Charles E. Townsend: *Russian Word Formation, corrected reprint*, viii + 272 p., 1975 (ISBN: 0-89357-023-0).

Janet G. Tucker: *Innokentij Annenskij and the Acmeist Doctrine*, 154 p., 1987 (ISBN: 0-89357-164-4).

Boryana Velcheva: *Proto-Slavic and Old Bulgarian Sound Changes*, Translation of the original by Ernest A. Scatton, 187 p., 1988 (ISBN: 0-89357-189-X).

Walter N. Vickery, ed.: *Aleksandr Blok Centennial Conference*, 403 p., 1984, (ISBN: 0-89357-111-3).

Essays in Honor of A. A. Zimin, ed. D. C. Waugh, xiv + 416 p., 1985 (ISBN: 0-89357-147-4).

Daniel C. Waugh: *The Great Turkes Defiance On the History of the Apocryphal Correspondence of the Ottoman Sultan in its Muscovite and Russian Variants*, ix + 354 p., 1978 (ISBN: 0-89357-056-7).

Susan Wobst: *Russian Readings and Grammatical Terminology*, 88 p., 1978 (ISBN: 0-89357-049-4).

James B. Woodward: *The Symbolic Art of Gogol: Essays on His Short Fiction*, 131 p., 1982 (ISBN: 0-89357-093-1).

Dean S. Worth: *Origins of Russian Grammar Notes on the state of Russian philology before the advent of printed grammars*, 176 p., 1983 (ISBN: 0-89357-110-5). (UCLA Slavic Studies, Volume 5)

Что я видел *What I Saw* by Boris Zhitkov, Annotated and Edited by Richard L. Leed and Lora Paperno, 128 p. (8.5 x 11" format), 1988 (ISBN: 0-89357-183-0).